Good Swimming

Good Swimming

Pathways to Better Swimming for Recreational and Lap Swimmers, Triathletes and other Competitors

Win Wilson

To order additional copies of this book, contact:
Xlibris Corporation
1-888-795-4274
www.Xlibris.com
Orders@Xlibris.com
59118

Credits

Foreword
: Donna de Varona

Technical Advisors
: Matt Kredich, Head Coach, Women's Swimming, University of Tennessee
: Edward Reed, Aquatics Director Emeritus, University of Alabama
: Jane Barkman Brown, Olympic Gold Medal Winner and Independent Swim Coach

Creative Workouts
: Richard H. Burrows, Esq., Former Head Swim Coach Dennison University

Photography and Video
: John Forasté — *www.foraste.com*

Illustrations
: Penny Jackim

Guest Photographer
: Peter H. Bick, After Image Photo — *www.peterbick.com*

Dedication

"It's sort of the last of the ninth inning, but I'm so far ahead
that I can't worry about losing."

The quote is from the late D. Barr Clayson, Brown University class of
1958, a New England Masters teammate. It's from a message he sent to
several of his friends a few weeks prior to his death in 2008. This book is
dedicated in his memory.

Despite a somewhat early passing, Barr lived a full and vibrant life, a life
filled with humor, good fun, and happiness. He was athletic, a swimmer of
near-Olympic caliber, a man to be envied for his looks, brains, success in
business, and lifestyle. He was, above all, a family man and someone who
lived his life always willing to give of himself. As might be expected, he had
many friends. I'm proud to have been one.

Acknowledgements

This book would not have been possible without the help and understanding of many friends and family members to whom I am very grateful. First was my wife of 46 years, Etta, now deceased, who encouraged me from the start. I wonder if she thought I would ever complete the project since it started so haltingly. She is greatly missed by me, her family, and friends.

A debt of extreme gratitude must also go to my good friend, the late John Jerome, an author for whom I had much regard. His life was writing and he did it with grace and style. He went over some of my earlier efforts with a very sharp red pencil, teaching me much. I was tremendously flattered when after reviewing an early draft of my almost-finished manuscript, he termed it an "important book." John is missed by his many friends and family.

Liza Collins, another wordsmith of some note, also took the time to read the manuscript and offered some fine suggestions that encouraged me to focus more on the needs of my audiences.

My good friend and companion, Ellen Mills, a sculptor and artist, has encouraged me in a quiet way. I learned from her to have confidence in what I was doing and to just keep plowing along with it. I'm grateful for her encouragement and suggestions, as well as for her excellent and always challenging company. And then there's her sister, Margaret (Mig) Tuchrello, a skillful writer and poet who read some of my material, and had many helpful thoughts.

Two other good friends, Nameer Jawdat, and the late Tom Lyndon, both writers, were willing to read what I had written and offer suggestions and encouragement.

Ed Reed, Matt Kredich, and Peter Brown, all highly knowledgeable professional coaches, read my manuscript with great care, providing me with a technical fail safe, not allowing me to wander too far out on the fringes of swimming technique and theory. I am very grateful to them, and to Peter, in addition, for the special help and advice he provided as the book developed. Another fine coach and friend, Jane Berkman Brown, a former Olympian, read a later version of the manuscript and provided a wealth of technical advice and helpful editing. Jane thought enough of my book to provide an endorsement. Ed, Matt and Jane all were willing to become official "technical advisors," for which I'm especially grateful.

Phil Whitten, my friend from Masters Swimming, Executive Director of the College Swimming Coaches Association of America, and former Editor of *Swim* Magazine, also read my manuscript and offered encouragement and helpful suggestions. His own book *The Complete Book of Swimming* has been a very useful resource.

I'm also grateful to Ernest Maglischo whose books, *Swimming Faster* and *Swimming Even Faster*, were both very useful resources. I'm grateful to Rick Pace, another friend and serious swimmer who offered many insights to the world of publication and who provided encouraging feedback as he utilized my book as he sought improvements in his own swimming.

I am especially grateful to my latter-day writing coach, Tom D'Evelyn, for his careful editing, concern and encouragement as we moved forward together on this project. He was always patient. His teaching upgraded my ability to write. Then, of course, there is Nan Hansen, who encouraged me to seek out Tom's help in the first place and then strongly encouraged me to publish.

I'm proud and pleased to have the support of folks like my good friend, John Forasté, the photographer for *Good Swimming*, my longtime friend and artist, Penny Jackim, whose sketches grace these pages, and my friends and professionals who provided endorsements—Jane Berkman Brown, John Conner, and Fred Bartlett. Then of course I must acknowledge my gratitude to Dave Paquin, Graham Newstead, and Amy Sexsmith, able swimmers, good friends, and wonderful training partners.

Richard Burrows, lawyer, friend, longtime swimmer, and in a past life a university coach of some significance, with whom I have had many technical discussions, has been most helpful. He generously furnished me with some of his creative workouts. These are found in the Appendix of *Good Swimming*.

I am grateful also to coaches John O'Neill, now at Providence College and Kevin Salisbury, at Community College of Rhode Island. Both have been helpful to me in many ways.

Tracy Grilli, longtime Administrator for U.S. Masters and an exceptional swimmer, has been of great help to me on numerous occasions, both for this book and in my often disorganized swimming life. She has always answered my requests for help, no matter how bizarre, efficiently and promptly with the good-natured friendliness that is her nature. She put me in touch with two other folks, Bill Volckening, USMS Editor and Peter Bick, a most creative photographer, who have been helpful as I sought pictures to enhance the book's graphics.

I have special feelings of gratitude for Donna de Varona, noted Olympian, double gold medal winner, TV analyst for swimming, and longtime advocate for women's sports, who read my book and offered to do the "Foreword" for its publication. I treasure her support.

By no means can I forget the fine folks at Xlibris, my publisher. Every time I turned around there was someone ready to help with wonderful efficiency. My initial editors, Miren Go and Apple Geradela, not only caught my many goofs but also provided with their notes a marvelous teaching file on the use of the comma and other niceties regarding the proper rules of the English language. There are so many fine people who helped me that a listing would be practically endless, but I am especially indebted to Karen Almendra for her capable help in steering *Good Swimming* along the path to production. And then there is the patient and creative Ray Usman, whose patience will be challenged, I'm sure, as we work together to market my book.

I cannot forget my able computer guru, Steve Putnam, who has received numerous panic calls from me and always managed to straighten me out.

I'm indebted to several assistant coaches at Brown University who have now gone on to other endeavors: Dan Shelley, Mike Lane and Deb Whitney. They were helpful to me in a number of ways, either in going over my material for technical flaws or in helping me and John Forasté as we did photography and video for *Good Swimming*. And it's hard to say enough in gratitude about John Forasté, who did so much beyond what would be expected of a photographer as he helped partner this book toward publication.

It's always dangerous to attempt to remember those who have helped. There are so many, and there is the danger of forgetting someone. There is my friend, Jim Edwards, who talked me into making a Masters comeback. There are those at Brown University, who have always been willing to let me use the pool. High on this list would be Arlene Gorton, longtime Associate Athletic Director. I also must not forget Dave Roach, who as Head Coach for Women at Brown, let me work out with his team and taught me the value and basics of weight training. Then, of course there was my first coach, the late Joe Watmough, who started me off on a lifetime swimming Odyssey that provided much in the formative structure of my life. So many individuals have helped: training partners; friends I've found in competitive venues throughout the world; numerous coaches and pool directors over the years who allowed me to swim or train with their teams in towns and cities around the country; and others, often in ways of which they were unaware. I am terribly grateful.

Foreword

Win and I have been discussing writing a book together on swimming for some time. We love the sport and both feel that learning how to swim has been a lifetime gift. When discussing the project with Win, I was intrigued with his approach. Unfortunately, considering my current workload and long-standing commitments made to various Olympic-related initiatives, I realized I could not make the kind of concentrated effort I knew it would take to partner with Win. However, after reading his first draft of *Good Swimming*, I told him I would support his dedicated effort any way I could.

Win has an excellent grasp for his material. I've been around the sport for more years than I'd want to admit. My love of the water began almost before I could walk, when my Dad would take me to the beach and dive into the crashing waves in San Diego, California, with me hanging onto his back. Later, I found I had a talent for racing when I attended a summer swim program at a local high school pool in Lafayette, California. Age-group swimming was taking hold in America then, and I was fortunate to find an excellent program. By the age of thirteen, I held my first world record and had become the youngest member of the 1960 Rome Olympic team. Four years later, I captured two gold medals at the Tokyo Olympics.

My swimming career opened up unimaginable doors for me. As an expert for my sport on ABC's *Wide World of Sports* and then later as a full-time broadcaster, I covered some seventeen Winter and Summer Olympics and, as such, was able to keep up with elite athletes and experts in a variety of fields, especially swimming. Currently a parent to two college students who love to swim, I have relived my competitive years while watching my son, John David Pinto, work his way up through the ranks of a YMCA age-group program to becoming a top-notch varsity swimmer for Brown University. In the summer, he competes in triathlons, where swimmers who can also run and bike have an advantage. My exposure has given me a keen awareness of coaching concepts.

Having said that, I can say without reservation that *Good Swimming* presents a wealth of valuable information designed to make all of us better swimmers. Win's approach has a crisp uniqueness that seems to be a fit for all ages. While written with the idea of making a reasonably adept swimmer better, there is much here for all—from aquatic neophytes to polished competitors. I would particularly recommend *Good Swimming* to triathletes who often need to perfect their swimming skills in order to improve overall performance.

Swimming is a dynamic and changing sport. During the 2008 Olympics in Beijing, Michael Phelps' successful attempt to capture eight Olympic gold medals in a single Olympics fueled unprecedented interest in swimming. In this sporting world where a plethora of sports compete for exposure, sponsorships, and TV time, swimming has emerged, at least during the Olympics, as the sport to watch. Over time, rule changes, which impact turns, strokes, and underwater work have aided in producing faster times. This year, however, technology gave birth to controversy when the buoyant fast swimsuit was given credit for the many world records set in international competitions. Many in the swimming world object to the price of the suit, $400 minimum, and feel that the suit should be banned because it artificially aids in enhancing performance. Where will it end? In a world where creeping commercialism has blurred the lines between amateur and professional sport and where new world records mean more exposure, which in turn attract sponsorships, it is not likely FINA, the swimming's world governing organization, will outlaw the suit.

Win is an accomplished swimmer in his own right; his swim times and records attest to success both in college and then in Masters competition. His love of the water and swimming come through loud and clear in *Good Swimming*. His ability to present teaching concepts in a way that makes one feel a coach is by your side explaining each step is a gift. It's a serious book written with the idea that the reader will learn from it. Yet there is a lighter element in the writing too as Win's sense of humor comes through on page after page.

A special quality I found in the book was Win's storytelling. His delightful vignettes never fail to present an important point, both in swimming and occasionally in life itself. It is a pleasure to recommend *Good Swimming* to anyone wanting to learn more about this unique sport.

Donna de Varona

Donna de Varona

Donna de Varona has been a swimming prodigy, world record holder, and the youngest member of the 1960 Olympics swimming team at the age of thirteen. She is also a holder of eighteen of the world's fastest times and was a double gold medalist in the 1964 Tokyo Olympics. In 1964, she was voted the Most Outstanding Woman Athlete in the world by Associated Press and United Press International and was also a Sullivan Award nominee. She was a pioneer Emmy Award–winning broadcaster for network sports and news television, covering Olympic swimming and other sports for many years. She often acts as a consultant to the US Senate for Olympic sports and Title IX legislation. She was the chair of the FIFA Women's World Cup and is an inductee of the International Swimming Hall of Fame, Olympic Hall of Fame, and National Women's Hall of Fame. She is a graduate of UCLA and is a holder of five honorary degrees. She is the mother of Joanna Pinto and John David Pinto.

CONTENTS

Section 3: Competition

Introduction

Over the years that I've been a Masters swim competitor, I've developed a number of informal coaching relationships with swimmers of various ages and skill levels. Along the way, I've taken a special interest in helping these people improve. *Good Swimming* is a natural outgrowth of what has become for me a strong coaching hobby.

In these years of avocational coaching, I learned that some of the best athletes I see in the pool aren't very good swimmers. I'm referring to triathletes. I have great admiration for these multiskilled athletes who so often ride their bikes or run, at what appears to me at least, excruciatingly long distances with a willingness to accept a high level of discomfort and even pain in order to improve their skills. I see many of these folks in the water. They work hard, but most are just not going at it the right way. A lot of them aren't that good. Oh, they're wonderful on the bicycle and track, but not so accomplished aquatically.

I've worked with a number of these men and women and have usually been rewarded to see big improvements as a result of my coaching. The really nice thing about working with the triathlon crowd is that they're invariably willing to put in the effort. They will work hard to improve! And sometimes, you don't even have to see them in the water to solve a problem.

On a trip a few years back, I met a budding triathlete, a man in his early forties, who told me his swimming was holding him back. He said he was a pretty good runner and biker, but he had no stamina for swimming. He was getting ready to quit trying to be a triathlete, and the idea of quitting was bothering him considerably. After some discussion, it became clear to me that he simply didn't know how to breathe properly while swimming. I mailed him my chapter on breathing, which at the time was in draft form. After some months, I received from him a ringing endorsement of the chapter. He wrote that he'd conquered his breathing problems and was now working out successfully with a Masters group. He'd put in a lot of work, but by following my instructions on breathing, he had been able to overcome the barrier that had been holding him back.

Obviously, I felt very good about being instrumental in his success. That's the joy in coaching even when it occurs from a distance. Realistically, however, whether it's from a distance or nearby, you can never absolutely guarantee anything. But with triathletes, many of whom are self-coached, I'm almost willing to say, "Read *Good Swimming*, it will help. I guarantee it!" Triathletes are among the group who will benefit the most from my book.

The other main audience I very much had in mind as I wrote is that amorphous group of men and women who loosely fall into the category of workout or lap swimmers. These folks go to the pool, many every day, and swim for a considerable distance. Very few of them are even self-coached. I see most of these people doing it the same way day after day, imprinting inefficient techniques into their neural/muscular systems. I always hesitate to blurt out an offering of advice, but sometimes I can't help myself. Generally, the advice is accepted in the spirit it is given, and some of these workout people actually get better. Swimming, like most sports, is a lot more fun when you do it right. The kinesthetic feedback you get in the water is an added dimension. You just plain feel better!

The book's focus at times will echo my empathy for the plight of the wannabe lap swimmer, the swimmer who has the desire but who lacks the know-how to achieve real exercise in the pool. To meet the needs of these folks, *Good Swimming* often goes back to basics—although to be sure, the basics are worth reviewing even for the more accomplished athlete. But many of the "wannabes" try hard to become true workout swimmers only to give up in frustration when improvement seems out of reach. These are the people who probably need help most, and it's a shame to see them drop out mainly because they do not have a source of simple, fundamental advice.

Those who do drop out end up missing a lot of fun and a wonderful form of exercise. But of course, swimming is much more than just another form of exercise. There's a special mystique in the act of swimming well. Swimmers are seen as people who have conquered what many consider a hostile environment. Unfriendly though it may be, the water we find in our pools, lakes, and oceans shouldn't be that unfamiliar to us. Our bodies are mostly water, and our first developing environment of the womb was primarily liquid. We should be comfortable in water, but we're not. Some of us hold it in outright fear. In any case, most would agree that the swimmer's environment is unique and swimmers, having at least partially conquered that environment, are a special breed. There's no question, but our more landlocked friends tend to see us that way.

This sense of specialness is a bond most swimmers feel. We don't think about it much, but it's there underneath the surface—the realization that we've somehow mastered an unfriendly medium and are therefore in a significant way different from those who haven't. And yet approached correctly, good swimming is not that hard to learn.

It's worth underscoring that the purpose of this book is simple and fundamental—to make the reader a better swimmer. The main focus will be on the front crawl, often referred to as freestyle. That's our most efficient stroke, the one that lap swimmers generally use in their swimming. It's the stroke of choice for more Masters swimmers than any other, and there are more freestyle competitive swimmers than specialists in other strokes. If a swim race calls for freestyle, it means that any stroke or combination of strokes may be used, but 99 percent of the time the event will be swum front crawl by all swimmers. Front crawl is the fastest, least energy-consuming way to swim. Marathon swimmers, such as English Channel challengers, almost always swim front crawl the whole distance.

Yet in order to be complete, there are chapters dissecting the basics of the other three competitive strokes: back crawl (backstroke), breaststroke, and that infamous, energy-burning way of swimming—butterfly. There will even be a word or two about sidestroke—not in itself on the competitive docket, but still a rather sedate form of swimming that has its adherents.

Knowing that most of my readers will be self-coached or even noncoached, in the writing I have as much as possible attempted to speak directly to the swimmer, much the way a coach on the pool deck would. I've tried to cut through all the technicalities and get right down to the simple fundamentals that will make you a better swimmer.

I've included as part of *Good Swimming* a number of short vignettes. While I had fun writing these little stories, they have a purpose. Each illustrates a point designed to make you a better athlete. You can think of them as aquatic parables. In addition, their purpose is to humanize and lighten the instructional material; in other words, to add to the fun of *Good Swimming*—yours and the book's.

I don't necessarily recommend reading the book straight through. The book is organized in three sections. *Section 1, "The Basics,"* is designed to be helpful to the beginner as well as the more advanced swimmer looking for a review. *Section 2, "Different Strokes and Other Information,"* provides a wealth of material aimed at helping the reader become a better swimmer in the noncrawl strokes. There are also a couple of chapters covering a more general aquatic background. *Section 3, "Competition,"* covers instructional material and tips for competitors and would-be competitors.

The chapter headings give a strong clue as to their content, and as a reader, you may already have a pretty good idea what your particular problem is in swimming. Still, as a note of caution, we need to remember that self-diagnosis can lead to faulty conclusions. The reason you're not swimming as well as you'd like may be quite different from what you thought. *Good Swimming*, because it is both comprehensive and basic, is a logical place to start the introspective process of dissecting what you're doing right and what you're doing wrong in the water.

My experience predicts that generally, readers seeking improvement will find the chapters on breathing and on use of the arms as the most relevant to their problems. Breathing errors while in the water and poor arm mechanics are the two most common problems I see in lap swimmers. And while the majority of triathletes have a pretty good handle on breathing, I see many who have fundamental flaws in their arm stroking. Often, the way to flush out old bad habits means a trip back to a proper beginning. In other words, back to basics. They're fully covered in *Good Swimming*.

Improvement in swimming, just as in any athletic skill, does not come easily. *Webster* defines a skill as "a developed or acquired ability." There's at least a hint in the *Webster* definition that some hard work may be required in acquiring a skill. Sometimes, hard work is mostly concentration, keeping your mind on what you're trying to accomplish. In other words, staying with it and at the same time trying new approaches to modify old habits. The aim of *Good Swimming* is to show some blueprints for doing just that. In any case, I've enjoyed writing the book. I hope it's helpful.

Special Preface for the Beginner

Good Swimming was written initially for the advanced swimmer. As I began writing, I realized that much of the material included in the book has valid application for the aquatic neophyte. Accordingly, it made sense to write this "special preface." My purpose is to provide instructions for beginners to bring their aquatic skills up to at least the intermediate level.

The special preface is short, and mastering the material presented here will take more time and effort than its reading. Even so, by diligently following the precepts and instructions presented in this section, the neophyte who is determined to become a swimmer, over several weeks, will have learned to swim. In fact, the art of basic swimming is a fairly simple process. Like most of what we learn in life, it just takes understanding and effort. So where do we start?

1. Overcoming Fear and Learning to Relax

When we began, most of us had a healthy respect for water, some of us an out-and-out fear. Respect is good, but fear must be conquered if you really want to learn to swim. Personally, and as a coach, I'm very uncomfortable when a nonswimmer approaches me for help and I suddenly realize he or she has a high fear quotient in the water. I then know we have to work on that problem first, and sometimes it's not easy. So overcoming fear is the first step in learning to swim.

One way to conquer fear is to get in the shallow end of the pool and literally play in the water. I remember telling my children, "Look, the water is your friend." While saying this, I would splash a little water, hold my breath, and duck under and tell them to do what I do. It's the same with adults who must for a few moments at least today—and maybe for several days—revert to childhood and play games in the water. Toys, balls, and the like can help. The idea is to concentrate on something other than being afraid. Have some fun; play a little. Learning to hold your breath and duck under for a few seconds is a very important early step. When the beginner ducks under the water's surface, it's best to use a well-fitting pair of goggles (see chapter 14, "Toys and Other Equipment"). That way, the beginner can start by keeping his/her eyes open, something that's important in the learning process. Competent swimmers almost always keep their eyes open while swimming even when their heads are facing down the water.

Another important aspect of overcoming fear is learning to relax in the water. Chapter 2 in this book, "Relaxing," can be helpful to all swimmers including the most basic beginners. Learning to float in the water is another way to enhance relaxing. Most humans can float, but I have seen a number of very competent swimmers who could not. So being able to float is not necessarily a requirement for swimming. Even a small amount of forward progress in the water will give the nonfloater the lift needed to keep on the surface. Being able to float does speed the learning along however. The best way to learn to float is to go to the shallow part of the pool, take a big breath of air, lean your head back, and just lie down in the water. Try to be totally relaxed. The gentle bobbing action in the water as you lift your feet and lie there is very pleasant.

Only you will know if you have made inroad toward overcoming your fear; one symptom of qualms you might not be aware of is tenseness in your body. Thus, at this point, it's important to do some introspective self-diagnosis. You should be able to judge just how relaxed you are in the water as you go through the playing and ducking under the surface I've suggested here. Tenseness and fear seem to go hand in hand with the beginner, but fear must be conquered and feelings of genuine relaxation established before the beginner can successfully move to the steps outlined below.

2. Leveling Out

Maintaining a horizontal position in the water is critical for a swimmer of any ability, but especially so for the beginner. So we must learn to level out—stay horizontal—in the water. There are a number of exercises that help us learn this skill.

One such drill is pushing off from the side of the pool under the surface of the water on your stomach, stretching out and gliding and trying to stay level just below the surface for as long as possible. Water about chest deep is ideal for this. The beginner should be able to stand up comfortably at this depth yet there should be enough water for the exercise.

Illustration shows the gliding position after push off from the wall.

The first step in this skill is to hold on to the side of the pool with one hand, then bring your legs into a tuck and place your feet about six inches below the level of the gutter. As you let go with the hand holding on to the gutter, push off with your legs, bring your holding hand forward, and ride both hands out in a horizontal position in front of your head slightly under the water. See how far you can go before your legs drop and you find yourself standing. At first, you will probably only be able to go a few feet. But keep at it. You will increase the distance you go on your push off as you become more skilled. When you do this drill, it's best to plant your feet sidewise on the side of the pool, parallel with the surface of the water. You then push off twisting your body into the facedown position for your glide. You will be able to get more thrust from your legs doing it this way.

This exercise is one you should do over and over, learning to coordinate the push off and then the stretching out and staying relaxed while you practice. Try to go as far as possible in the glide. At first, even one body length of glide may be a challenge, but remember, experienced swimmers can glide for two or more body lengths. This skill will serve you well as you move on to higher levels in your aquatic ability.

Once you've become comfortable with the push off and glide skill, it's time to add some basic arm action. Here, I recommend a reading of chapter 4, "The Key Is in Your Arms." Obviously as a beginner, you cannot expect to have elegant, efficient arm action, but it's time to start.

After reading the chapter and achieving a basic understanding of how your arms are supposed to work in swimming, give it a try in the water. After you push off and glide for a few feet, start with one arm and then the other. Keep your head down. Don't even try to add breathing action. That will come later. It's best to start with two strokes—one for each arm. Then stand up in the water. Do it again, this time trying for three or four strokes. Be careful. Keep your head down and eyes open. Stay in the shallow water. When you're able to do about six strokes (three for each arm), you're ready to try kicking.

3. Kicking

Here again, my advice is to read chapter 5, "The Flutter Kick for Freestyle." This material will give you the basics you need to know as to the mechanics of what kicking is all about. Throughout *Good Swimming*, I emphasize that our arms provide most of the propulsion for our swimming. Even so, learning a solid kicking motion that will repeat without your having to think about it is an invaluable skill in swimming. In other words, kicking should be automatic.

The best approach for this is to use a kickboard. Start with the biggest one you can find. Almost all recreational pools will have them around. Get into the chest-deep water in the pool, hold the board between your arms, gripping at the far end, then push off holding the board in front of you. Stay level in the water and start your kicking action. If you're having trouble coordinating all this new action, you can always go to the side of the pool, grip the gutter while on your stomach, and once again, while stretching out, start kicking.

These new kicking motions won't necessarily come easily, but with practice, you will improve. Furthermore, you now have a number of skills you can work on. Some coaches think that kicking is the way to start the learning process. I see it as critically important but believe for most learners that the order listed in this special preface is more logical. But now is the time to review everything you have learned so far. It can be helpful to go to the pool with a list of the skills you are going to work on. Go right back to the beginning. Float a little. Do some push offs, both just gliding and with the arm action. Try your kicking. Push off with your head down and start your kicking action. Just as competitive swimmers break their skills down and work on them in a unique fashion—for arms, the use of paddles and pull buoy; for kicking, the use of a board and sometimes even fins—you now have enough skills to work on, breaking out separate aspects of what you have learned with plenty of things to review before you move ahead. When you're comfortable and feel you have mastered these steps, you are ready to move forward with your swimming.

Another way to learn your kicking is to combine it with floating. Lie down in the shallow water and go into your float; then without too much violent splashing, move your legs into the kicking motion. Try to stay relaxed. You're on your back now, but kicking is the same for both front crawl and backstroke. This is another approach to learning to swim that many coaches favor. It's good to practice this skill along with the other aspects of swimming that you're now learning.

4. Putting Things Together

This is just the basics. A much more comprehensive discussion of coordinating the various skills needed for swimming is found in chapter 6, "Bringing It All Together: Breathing, Arms, and Kick." The missing ingredient for the beginner at this point is, of course, the all-important skill of learning to breathe while swimming. We're not ready for that just yet however. Right now, the need is to get your arms and kick working in a somewhat coordinated manner as you employ a good, strong push off from the side of the pool in water shallow enough for standing.

It's really fairly simple. Push off and begin your glide. Keep your head down—holding your breath, of course—and start your kick, and at the same time begin your arm stroke as before. You've got a lot to think about, and that's why it's important to have a kick that's pretty much "automatic" and why you need to do lots of kicking with the board and while gliding. For a good swimmer, everything becomes automatic after a while, but it takes lots of practice.

Obviously, you're not going to go very far in the water if you're doing all your swimming (and yes, you're actually swimming now) with your face down in the water, holding your breath. So if you've been doing lots of practice, you're getting pretty comfortable in the water—your arm action is reasonably long and strong, your kick is getting automatic, and you're able to take four or five strokes (each arm)—then it's time to take that big leap forward: learning to breathe while you swim. Chapter 1 in *Good Swimming* is titled "In the Beginning There Is Breathing" for good reason. Once a person progresses beyond just the pure basic stage, the ability to breathe while swimming is what makes the difference between a real swimmer and someone who is just able to paddle around a bit. So at this point, you can be your own judge; if you're ready, it's time to move on. If in your judgment you're not yet ready, you need more practice on the basic skills outlined here. For the beginner ready to move on, breathing is outlined in chapter 1.

Section 1

The Basics

Chapter 1

In the Beginning There Is Breathing

This chapter is basic. Most accomplished lap swimmers can probably skip it. On the other hand, breathing problems are often the bane of even good swimmers. Note the italicized sentence in the third paragraph below. That's the self-test for this chapter. If you can't pass it, this chapter may be helpful.

Whenever I'm in a small group, the discussion sooner or later turns to swimming. Despite what my New England Masters teammates say, I really don't force these conversations. They just happen. And then invariably, someone will offer a comment like, "You know, I'm a pretty good swimmer, but after one length, I'm really exhausted."

Well, normal, healthy men and women, even middle-aged or older men and women, don't get really exhausted after twenty-five yards of swimming if they're doing it right. So when I hear statements like this, I generally take a closer look at the source. If the speaker has all the arms and legs stuck at all the right places and otherwise appears reasonably healthy, then I'm 99 percent sure I know what the problem is—breathing!

Let's face it. There's no way any of us can enjoy lap swimming or any kind of open-water distance swimming until we solve the basic problem of breathing. *The goal for the would-be swimmer has to be to breathe as naturally while swimming as when walking.* Once you pass the breathing hurdle, the horizons of what you can do in the water will expand explosively. And learning to do it right is not that difficult.

It's a goal worth restating—you want to be able to breathe as naturally in the water as out of it. That's the minimum objective for any would-be lap swimmer. With practice, proper breathing will become a perfectly natural skill—a reflex really! Today, after years of swimming, I never think about breathing except of course at the end of high-intensity training sets or after finishing an all-out race when a price must be paid. Then I'm truly gasping for air. But when moving along at a comfortable pace, my breathing is very natural. I don't give it a thought. I remember one day not too many years ago doing some long, easy swimming and feeling so loose and natural in the water that for a moment I literally forgot my environment. Coming out of a turn, I caught myself about to take a nice, big breath while still at least a foot beneath the surface. It wasn't in any sense a gasping or struggling action out of need for air, but rather a simple lack of attention, forgetting for a moment where I was. That breath I almost took would surely have been a problem. Gills I haven't developed yet!

But even advanced swimmers sometimes have breathing problems. One of my good friends who has been competing for a long time has a chronic, but not uncommon, bad habit of *not getting rid of all his air.* The result is a carbon dioxide buildup and breathlessness. A sign for diagnosing this particular breathing flaw in a swimmer is a show of redness in the shoulders, upper arms, and back. My friend has developed a unique safety valve I do not recommend. Doubling up on his breathing, he takes quick breaths on each side, left and right, literally panting his way through workouts and races. Luckily, he has a smooth stroke and gets away with this fairly well. Coaches have been telling him about the problem for years, but he has never confronted the flaw, opting instead for compensation—double breathing.

The cure would be quite simple—greater emphasis on exhaling. For my friend with long-standing poor mechanics now ingrained in his system, the change would take special emphasis and concentration. The payback, however, would be faster races, even as he moves along in his golden years, and far more comfortable swimming especially at stressful speeds and distances.

Breathing on land is a natural, involuntary action. The diaphragm relaxes, allowing the lungs to expand and accept air through the nose. The diaphragm contracts, constricting the lungs and forcing them to expel air. In and out! In and out! It happens all the time, and we hardly think about it. The involuntary action of breathing can speed up or slow down by our body's demand. We can "reach way back" when we want an especially big one that fills a great deal more of our lungs. We're in the nice, friendly land atmosphere of 20 percent oxygen, and we just breathe and take it for granted.

But breath means life. Our bodies take in oxygen to be "burned," making our systems go. We expel the waste product of burning: carbon dioxide. Our lungs are the critical pathways to life where the exchange of oxygen and carbon dioxide in our blood takes place. (A little more thought about this basic physiology and some of our friends who smoke might have second thoughts about the long-term damage they do to themselves.)

On land, breathing is a simple in and out. In water, new skills must be learned. The singsong drill for what we used to call artificial respiration comes to mind: "Out goes the bad air, in comes the good!" A litany for rhythm as we practiced the old prone/push method in life-saving training.

In the water, this is key—"out goes the bad air!" But it doesn't just go out. We've got to *force it out* from the deep resources of our chests. This is critical. Air must be forced out hard while the mouth and nose are underwater. A good line of bubbles should flow from your nose and mouth. You should feel you're forcing nearly all the air out of your lungs with the expelling action. Then when your head returns to the side and your mouth opens, all you'll need is a quick "bite" of air. Remember, *all* the "bad air" that goes out is forced out underwater.

My friend's error of not getting rid of all the bad air—carbon dioxide—underwater is common. Trying to exhale and then inhale at the same time can't be done with any success for long. To put it another way, when your head turns to the side for a breath, you've got to be ready to take in air. The result of three or four cycles of trying to take in air while you're still carrying a lungful is you are really exhausted.

There's a very simple exercise that can work for anyone having trouble developing good breathing habits. I call it bob breathing. Simply go to a corner in the deep end of the pool and start bobbing. With both hands on the gutter, take a breath and immediately duck underwater, expelling air as you do. Be sure to expel *all* the air. Bob to the surface by pulling yourself up with your hands and suck in a *quick bite* of air. Try to get into a nice, smooth rhythm. Keep this up until you can repeat for at least one hundred breaths. It should be comfortable and natural. Don't force it. If you're having trouble with the rhythm, stop and catch your breath. Take a break, but be sure to think through what you're supposed to be doing. Then start over. Once you've got it going right, practice this exercise daily for a while and then work on transferring this new breathing skill to your swimming. It should happen easily.

If you're still having trouble, try another very basic exercise. Stand chest high in some water, preferably the shallow end of your pool, and, while standing on the bottom, bend over so that your mouth, nose, and eyes approximate the position they would be in while swimming. In other words, the waterline on your face and head should run from just above your eyebrows across the tops of your ears to the back of your head. From this position, force the air out of your mouth and nose underwater, then without picking your head up, simply turn it to your breathing side and take a quick breath. Immediately turn your face back to its original position under the surface and again *force the air out*. Keep repeating this until you can do one hundred breaths with no trouble.

In this exercise, you're mimicking the head position for actual swimming, and many learners find this a natural progression. Both exercises allow you to isolate the specific breathing skill you're learning without the complication of the other body movements required to propel yourself forward in the water.

The key is to really force that air out underwater. Sometimes we learn by example. There is my old memory of watching Forbes Norris, then American long-distance champion, working out. Handicapped with a leg problem, Norris had developed a tremendous shoulder and arm action. But what struck me that day was the noise. A loud grunt reverberated through the small pool, building each time Norris exhaled. It was like watching and *listening to* some strange aquatic mammal working its way back and forth, making those sounds of quick, energetic breathing. I've never heard anyone else exhale quite so loudly and forcefully. Generally, when swimmers exhale underwater, it's a silent action, but Norris was exhaling with violence. For me, this was a vivid example of the force needed for getting rid of air underwater. Luckily, I had just happened by when Norris was concentrating on his breathing. But the point was driven home, and I became a better swimmer because of it.

Let's assume you have now learned to get rid of your air underwater but you're still having problems when you try to apply this new skill to actual swimming. Many people have trouble making the transition from breathing-exercise drills to breathing properly while swimming. Mostly it's just a question of doing it—that old bugaboo—practice! The key transition drill is the second one outlined above where you practice turning your head to the side to get your bite of air.

It's important to remember to keep the motion simple, just a turning of the head and shoulders. The common mistake I see is head lifting during the breathing cycle. That's a serious error. Lifting your head while swimming changes your body position and creates a number of flaws that make swimming more difficult. You really don't need to lift your head to get that breath. In fact, the forward motion as you swim will make breathing easier. And the faster you go, the easier it gets. Once you discover the proper amount of head turn needed, you'll find that a small air pocket will form in the water around your mouth. This happens as your forward momentum creates a small wave around your face and mouth. The air pocket is created behind the wave. This is where the air you'll breathe will come from.

Remember, don't lift your head. Just turn it laterally; at the same time, roll your body to enhance your head turn as you pull with the opposite arm (nonbreathing side). Other chapters will go into this more deeply, but normal front crawl swimming demands a certain amount of body roll. In order to keep this rotation equal, left and right, many coaches teach their younger athletes to breathe on both sides (bilateral breathing), the breathing pattern being: breathe, skip the breath for a complete stroking cycle, then breathe again on the opposite side. Not too many of us older folks can do this. We need our air too badly, but bilateral breathing is a marvelous way of ensuring even stroking, thus eliminating hitches and other stroke abnormalities.

This ties into the problem of discovering your normal breathing side. That's a tough question. I'm right-handed almost to an extreme, but I normally breathe to the left. I can breathe to the right, but it's never been truly comfortable. The advice is to try it on both sides and go with the one that feels most normal to you. Still, I'd recommend practicing on both left and right even after you've decided which one is normal for you. And remember, bilateral breathing tends to smooth out stroke mechanics, thus reducing the chance of gross errors in stroking that can occur when all breathing takes place on one side.

Breathing is without question the fundamental building block that must carry the rest of our swimming skills. If we are unable to breathe comfortably while swimming, there is no way we can make progress as the aquatic animals we'd like to be. It's therefore an absolute necessity for anyone hoping to be a good workout swimmer that these breathing skills be learned to the point of second nature. And it's not really that difficult. Good luck!

Chapter 2

Relaxing

Many lap swimmers seem very tense. A sense of relaxation is critical for good swimming. This chapter contains some thoughts and ideas to help you improve your ability to be relaxed as a swimmer.

A proper sense of relaxation in your swimming and good feel for the water are closely related. Coaches are always telling their swimmers to relax as they swim, and they talk a lot about developing a feel for the water, something you can't develop easily unless you go about it in a relaxed way.

Thinking back to my own early days of swimming, I know I had as much difficulty with relaxation as the next guy. My main issue in the beginning was breathing. That and outright fear of this new unfriendly environment my mother was about to launch me into. That's a common denominator. We all like to breathe, and when we're first in the water, it seems as though there's no way we can manage it. As a result, we tense up. That makes learning to swim very difficult.

Learning to relax and learning to breathe in the water usually come hand in hand. It certainly worked that way for me. As a young boy, I learned to breathe by keeping my head up and turning it from side to side as I stroked. This wasn't elegant, but I see a lot of youngsters swimming the same way today. It's a logical first step for many of us who didn't get much decent instruction.

The next steps for me were the imaging process. I was fortunate enough to spend a couple of summers at a boy's camp in New Hampshire where there were several older campers who swam well. I watched what they were doing and tried to emulate. It worked, and as I got better, I relaxed more and then improved even more. By the time I got to college, I wasn't by any stretch polished, but I was comfortable in the water and quite relaxed. The coaching was first-rate, adjustments were made to my breathing, relaxation was emphasized, I improved a great deal, and before long I was a polished swimmer competing successfully for my school.

This really leads to the following key questions: How do you relax? And what can you do to improve your sense of relaxation in your swimming?

Relaxation Practice on Land

Most people are apprehensive when they first think about getting into the water. These are natural feelings. Humans are land animals; any relationships to fish go way back in time. So naturally, we must consider our comfort level in the water. If you're pretty comfortable there, you shouldn't have any real problems with learning to be more relaxed. But if you're just not all that comfortable in the water, then some relaxation practice on land should be helpful. Start by sitting in a chair or lying on a couch or bed. This relaxation drill can be almost hypnotic. Let your mind tell each of your limbs to relax, just let go—no muscular effort at all. Then start by tensing one arm, being sure the remainder of your body is completely at rest and relaxed. Now let the tense arm relax and tighten the muscles in the other arm. Do the same thing with each leg.

While you're doing this simple exercise—running it through five to ten times—be sure to register in your mind the feelings of relaxation versus those of muscular effort. That's what relaxation is all about—the lack of muscular activity. The mind plays a critical role here too. It's difficult to maintain any sense of physical relaxation if the mind is tense and overloading your body with tension signals.

The ability to relax allows us to sleep, and when the mind is unduly active because of stress or perhaps simply because we're dwelling on life's problems while in bed, tension can be created that runs counter to the feelings of relaxation that lead to sleep. Hard physical exercise, such as found in running or swimming, can help us overcome this syndrome of tension. We're somehow able to flush out the tenseness through hard muscular and aerobic activity. But not if done too close to bedtime!

Relaxation in the Pool

The kind of relaxation we're seeking in swimming is a little different. *You've got to learn to relax one set of muscles while another set is working hard.* For some folks, this is not easy. As an example, I see lots of pretty good swimmers who, when using their kickboards, rock back and forth, dipping their shoulders from side to side as they kick. This is a sign of upper body tension, the lack of relaxation in the upper body while the muscles of the legs and lower body are working. Those who can relax are able to maintain level shoulders as they kick.

Back to learning to relax. After you've run through the land exercise outlined earlier and feel you've mastered it, meaning you now have a pretty good kinesthetic sense for the difference between muscular tension in a limb and its relaxation, it's time to take the drill to the pool. Start in the shallow end. It's easier to have confidence when you're in the shallow end. Put yourself in a floating position on your back. Just as you did before in your chair or on the bed, relax. Let the tension go out of your muscles. Just lie there in the water. Try to feel and enjoy the water that surrounds you. This sense of pleasure will help you relax. Then go through the procedure of tensing one limb at a time while the rest of your body maintains its completely relaxed state. It should come with a little practice, providing you're comfortable in the water and can float. Nonfloaters will have trouble with this exercise, but there are other drills in this chapter that can help. And it definitely isn't necessary to be able to float in order to swim in a relaxed way.

Relaxation while Kicking

In the chapter "The Flutter Kick for Freestyle," I emphasize the importance of keeping everything below the knee relaxed for a good kick. I underscore the importance of ankle relaxation. Of course, it's an advantage to have good flexibility in the ankles so that you have a good range of motion for effective kicking. Even having a good range of motion, however, won't do you much good if you don't also have the ability to relax the lower leg and ankle as you kick.

In a drill I've used to teach proper relaxation in the kick, the swimmer goes to the edge of the pool where the water is at least five feet deep. The swimmer holds on to the edge of the pool at the gutter and maintains a vertical position, facing horizontally along the poolside. Next, the swimmer goes through the kicking motion, gently with the outside leg.

The swimmer should be able to look down into the water to see what she is doing. If done correctly, with the leg nicely relaxed, the swimmer will note and feel the bend at the knee as the leg is pressed forward. She will feel the water pressure on the top of her foot and see the foot point in the water. As the leg is pressed toward the rear, she will see the leg straighten and the foot return to a less-pointed position. In this drill, the swimmer should seek that relaxed feeling in the lower leg and feel the pressure of the water against both the lower leg and foot while the big thigh muscles are doing the work.

Arm Relaxation

Relaxation in the arms is important also, particularly in recovery. The power phase in the arms uses fairly hard muscular activity; but this action of the muscles of the chest, back, and arms as the stroke, after entry, goes to the stretch, catch, outsweep and insweep phases, changes after the upsweep and release. Now those muscles should relax while the muscles of the shoulder work to bring the arm through the recovery phase. And very little muscular activity is necessary to make the recovery. Here are some exercises that can help you learn to relax on recovery.

One is the "floppy arm drill." Here, you simply swim normally, but after the release of each stroke near the bottom of your suit, bring your arm back through the recovery phase in a relaxed way. Let it be totally loose and flop into the water in front of your head. Try to feel a complete sense of relaxation in the recovering arm as you swim.

Another drill I like is the "high elbow, finger drag drill." (See the chapter "The Key Is in Your Arms.") You simply swim in a normal fashion except you lift your elbows on recovery and drag your fingertips across the surface of the water. Your hand and lower arm should be relaxed as you do this drill. This is a wonderful drill to teach both relaxation and feel for the water.

Relaxation and Technique

Relaxation will come as you develop technique. Technique and relaxation are inseparable, and as such they are self-supporting. Remember, your aim is to learn to swim with grace and power. I comment elsewhere in this book on the "flowing effortlessness" we think of in good swimming. A skilled athlete is able to apply force coupled with relaxation to save energy, which will only be expended in the most efficient way. The flowing effortlessness comes about through relaxation and developing a good feel for the water. This is where you learn to blend with your liquid environment, feeling it, enjoying it, and somehow almost becoming part of it as you move through it.

Chapter 3

Imaging

For a lot of folks who want to swim better, this might be the most important part of the whole book. Imaging can be the first step in swimming breakthroughs. Ideally, it's a kinesthetic shortcut to good swimming.

Imaging is a useful skill for any budding athlete. It is the ability to look at the action of someone and then duplicate that action for yourself. It requires a very special kind of concentration. This is no panacea for the instant acquisition of motor skills but rather the application of a concentration technique that speeds the learning process.

I find imaging very useful, not only in swimming but also in every sport I've tried. Even so, it's particularly applicable to a sport that involves repetitive movements. My late New England Masters teammate John Jerome, in his book *The Sweet Spot in Time,* delves rather deeply into the subject of acquiring new skills in the chapter entitled "Grooves." The following is according to Jerome:

> **For starters, you have to pay attention. You have to be engaged by the problem; you have to come at it with a level of mental and sensory arousal sufficient to pick up the stimulus cues you need for a solution.**
>
> *Next you will probably examine the problem by comparing it with your own experience, scanning your past for similar applicable skills that might provide alternative solutions, assessing your own*

capacities and how they might apply. You make a series of more or less unconscious judgements about where your movements must take effect, about the speed of movement, the space, the force required. You will probably go through a certain amount of covert rehearsal complete with spoken instructions to yourself—vocal or subvocal—depending on the complexity of the task.

*Then you attempt the movement, running a constant comparison check between the motions you intend and the motions you are constantly making, correcting the differences. As the discrepancy is reduced, as you grow confident that you can accomplish the movement you have in mind, you are able to reduce the monitoring and let your attention go on to other things. This is where the movement begins to become a skill. In your first fumbling attempts—complete with instructions to yourself—the higher brain centers are in almost total control, leaving very little for any other controlling mechanism to do. **As you are able to stop, consciously analyzing every aspect of the motion, the higher brain centers begin to tune out. In effect, you acquire a skill by taking the act out of your head and putting it away neurologically in your spine.*** (The bold italics are my notations.)

Ideally, what you want to do with imaging is suggested by the *bold italics* at the beginning and end of the quote—implying the mental gymnastics of a jump from the first bold italics to the second. In other words, keeping what Jerome refers to as the "higher brain" out of the learning process as much as possible. I often catch myself referring to my imaging as "going to school on someone," a laid-back expression learned from days when more time was spent on the golf course than in the pool.

As Jerome suggests, imaging involves both the conscious and the unconscious. The goal is to get the correct repetitive movements needed for swimming or for that matter, any sport ingrained into your neuromuscular system so you don't have to think about them. Obviously, if you're going to do effective imaging aimed at making you a better swimmer, you have to know the differences between good and bad technique. I make this point again later in this chapter, but it's critically important to have a good model for your imaging. A swim coach, if available, can help with this. Even a knowledgeable, highly competent fellow swimmer can be helpful. And then this book itself provides a wealth of material that will help you to discriminate between the correct and the not so correct in swimming.

At this point, there is an implication that your swimming, at least in some regard, needs improvement. Some hard introspection is called for so that you can properly define what it is more specifically that you need to work on. Here again, a coach or fellow swimmer can usually be helpful. This step involves defining the problem.

Once the problem has been properly defined, it is helpful to break down Jerome's quote in a step-by-step paraphrase:

1. *Pay attention.* Focus all your thoughts on the person and action you are observing! This part is really critical. You need to empty your mind of everything except the swimmer you are focusing on. It sounds simple and, for many of us, it comes naturally, but other folks have to work at it.

    The concept of emptying your mind gets us close to Zen Buddhism. Shunryu Suzuki, the great Zen master, in his book *Zen Mind, Beginner's Mind* speaks of composure, of having a calm mind, so that you can see and feel things as they are without any effort. In his words,

    > *When you have something in your consciousness, you do not have perfect composure. The best way toward perfect composure is to forget everything. Then your mind is calm, and it is wide and clear enough to see and feel things as they are without any effort. The best way to find perfect composure is not to retain any idea of things whatever they may be—to forget all about them and not to leave any trace or shadow of thinking.*

    So when Jerome or I say, "Pay attention," it often takes some serious mental effort to flush out your mind to ready it to accept the new concept you are dealing with. In reality, it's almost a two-step process. You need to empty your mind so that you can then give all your attention to focusing on your swimmer model.

2. *Compare what you are seeing with what you now do.* What are the differences in what you're seeing and what you normally do? This step once again takes immense concentration. You will think through the way you have been swimming, trying to break your stroke down to

smaller components, comparing these movements to what you are now seeing in the subject of your imaging. You will need to think through your own skills to understand where you will be able to apply this new way of swimming.

3. *Judgments.* What in your swimming needs to change? Think this through carefully. Make decisions about what you will change and what you will change it to—your imaging model. So the judgments you'll be required to make in this step involve the actions you now make, but that you'll want to change in order to get your own swimming closer to the ideal as represented by your imaging model.

4. *Try it out.* This can be frustrating. You will be making new motions at the same time doing a running comparison between what your new moves are and what you're visualizing. In this trial period, you may need some help from a knowledgeable friend or coach. What you think you're doing may not come close to the model upon which you were imaging. In this period of trial and error, you'll be making constant corrections. The more effective you are at the visualization, the quicker you will be able to reduce the discrepancies between what you are doing and the ideal—your model swimmer.

5. *Moving the conscious brain out of it.* At this point, you begin to get it right, and you stop thinking about it. As Jerome says in the last line I quoted, "You acquire a skill by taking the act out of your head and putting it away neurologically in your spine."

If you really concentrate and take each of the steps outlined here, imaging should happen. It may not happen quickly or all at once. I advise patience. The changes are worth waiting for, and they can happen at a level best described as "magical."

A few years back, this magical realization happened to me during a summer ocean workout. As a sometime distance competitor, I had long been envious of the modern-day, college-level distance swimmers who rip through the water in a style that appears almost effortless. I knew what set them apart: the two-beat energy-efficient crawl.

The two-beat kick allows the swimmer to emphasize arm action for greater stroke efficiency over longer distances where more aerobic (oxygen burning) effort is required. The two-beat style means that the swimmer kicks twice for each complete (both sides) arm revolution. It's easier to visualize it as one kick on each side for each arm stroke on the same side. The more classic and perhaps more natural six-beat kick involves three kicks per individual arm stroke—six for the full-arm cycle of both arms. The best I had been able to manage toward the two-beat was a clumsy, leg-dragging kind of swimming. Even this allowed me to go faster over longer yardages than I could manage with my more natural six-beat stroke, but it was far from ideal.

For some time, I had been mentally dissecting the two-beat fine-looking kick rhythms of the better swimmers on both the men's and women's teams at Brown University where I work out. My mental gymnastics were done mostly out of a mix of curiosity and envy. Deep down, I had some nagging, old-dog doubts that I'd ever be able to switch over to a two-beat nice, smooth mechanism after so many years and thousands of miles of six-beat action. Even so, without even knowing it, I had emptied my mind of envy and doubt and concentrated on what these good swimmers were doing. It was once again my old trick of studying someone else's expert athletic action to learn it for myself.

That summer a few years ago, I had my imaging epiphany. The day was sparkling, one of those midsummer mornings when it is a special joy to be alive. It was late morning with no wind and a dead-calm sea. I was swimming along parallel to the shore, moving fairly well, having logged about one thousand yards of mixed strokes for a good warm-up. All of a sudden, something clicked as I began to swim with more purpose. I could feel my legs working in a way that was new, yet at the same time vaguely familiar. My stroke had a nice, smooth lift, a little less pressure on the arms, and I seemed to be moving unusually fast for the effort I was putting into it. The feeling lasted for two or three hundred yards before fatigue and reality set in.

This was my first experience with a new way of swimming—my very own two-beat kick! Now years later, my two-beat kick does a pretty effective job for me. It's still not as defined or as strong as I'd like it, but it feels very natural. Today, as I move through my seventies, my pace in swimming events has slowed; but right after learning this new skill, my distance times improved dramatically, and I began to actually enjoy the previously dreaded longer freestyle events. I'm sure my teammates suspected I was either taking steroids or had discovered the Fountain of Youth. Actually, all I really had discovered was that I could do the two-beat kick.

And it was a discovery made kinesthetically. It didn't just happen although it certainly seemed that way at the time. I had made it happen. Even though the thinking part of my brain did not learn for a long time when and what I should be doing with my legs in relation to the motions of my arms, by closely observing—imaging—my body learned what to do.

This past year, I've been working out with a friend who's my junior by some fifteen years. He puts me away when we swim together or use the kickboard, but once we put the hand paddles on and go at it, I've been king. Then just the other day, I found I had to really turn on the steam just to stay at his feet. When we completed our "pull" set, I congratulated him. He replied that he'd found a "secret weapon," and he went on to say, "You know, Win, I've been behind you while we were pulling, but I've been watching you. It finally clicked in for me what you were doing. I saw how there was a little pause when your arms were under your body, and then you really pushed back. I tried it today for the first time, and it really worked!" (In reality, the hand does not pause under the body although there is that appearance as your hand changes direction, and its movement shifts from a pulling action to a pushing action.)

My friend's breakthrough was a vivid example of imaging in action. Imaging engages a very basic "kinesthetic system" where the body—nerves, muscles, tendons, all the body tissue that makes us move—takes over on its own. The nervous system is critical. The kinesthetic system feels its way to the most efficient athletic movement. This develops through the very special concentration required of the imaging technique. Usually, improvements come gradually. And yet sometimes there is a "clicking in," and the learning athlete suddenly realizes something different is happening; it just feels a whole lot better.

Anyone about to try this technique should know exactly what to image on. Imaging on a poor model is, of course, counterproductive. Instead of good habits, bad habits can be indelibly stamped into your system. You have to know what to look for. Actually, it's relatively easy to find good swimmers to pattern yourself after, but it's important to remember that even good swimmers often have stroke idiosyncrasies that are nonproductive. These stroke aberrations are often highly visible and invitingly easy material for imaging. It is critically important to be discriminating in your choice of models. Know or get advice on good and bad before setting in motion your own powers of dissection and concentration. *Good Swimming*, with its descriptions and visuals, is designed to help you to be discriminating. In applying the lessons found here, not only will you improve your own swimming directly, but you'll also learn a great deal that will be helpful as you seek the best real-life models for imaging.

But some folks just seem to have trouble reaching the end of the five-step imaging process I outlined earlier. If that sounds like you, don't give up. Combine it with other pathways to improve your swimming. John Forasté, the photographer for *Good Swimming*, is not only an excellent photographer, but also a pretty good swimmer. He's planning at least one ocean marathon this summer. Even so for some time, he's been working on a major stroke defect. It's his arms. His is a case of pulling out short at the end of his stroke combined with the ever-insidious "dropped elbows"—something you'll hear more about in *Good Swimming*. Unfortunately, he's been doing it his way for a long time—probably more than forty years.

But with his marathon attempt in mind, we've been working on his stroke in hopes of improving his swimming efficiency. The imaging technique doesn't seem to work well for John. He says he sees it—someone's more elegant stroke—and he understands it, but converting what he sees and understands to his own neuromuscular system just isn't happening for him. He's made it through steps number 1, 2, and 3 outlined earlier in this chapter, but he's stuck somewhere on step number 4.

Perhaps the visual orientation he uses in his professional life as a photographer has resulted in a certain understanding that comes so quickly that the images don't have time to filter down to his neuromuscular system. That's just a guess on my part. But what he's got going for himself is a marvelous desire to improve and a willingness to work at it. He's following a whole range of exercises and drills of the kind explained in *Good Swimming*. And suddenly, he's making progress. At times, his swimming has taken on a new longer and more graceful look, and you can see his excitement in his new way of swimming.

With John, imaging has been only a partial pathway to better swimming. I suspect that's the way it will be for many swimmers. Magical, mystical breakthroughs will happen only occasionally. But even in John's case, the imaging that I have harped on with him has been a useful adjunct to the other coaching methodologies we have used.

We learn to accept each step at a time, but the more we practice, the more quickly progress will come; and who knows, you may be one of the fortunate ones who learn easily and quickly through the imaging process—in other words, a coach's dream athlete. But even if you're not one of these gifted athletes, I recommend the imaging process to you. Even partial success with it, like John's, can be a big help.

Chapter 4

The Key Is in Your Arms

This chapter covers materials suited for both advanced swimmers and those not so advanced. It becomes fairly technical but is critically important for better swimming.

Don Cameron was one of my good friends on my college team. He and I had lots of off-the-record events we made up, little contests like underwater swimming, length of push off, kicking races—just about anything that might make our competitive juices flow. One day, he suggested that he could go under a minute for one hundred yards, just using his arms. Since Don's best time for the one hundred freestyle swimming all out was just under fifty-five seconds (a pretty good time back in the 1950s), his boast didn't sound reasonable to me at the time.

After some negotiation—I wanted to give myself a little margin—I challenged him to a $5 bet that he couldn't break fifty-eight seconds swimming with just his arms. He accepted my challenge and allowed me to put a couple of tight inner-tube sections around his ankles so that he would be unable to kick. To my amazement, Don did the one hundred in a tick under fifty-six seconds, even surprising himself somewhat. The $5 I lost was money well spent because it taught me a valuable lesson in the critical importance of arm action in swimming. Later on, I tried doing the same thing, an all-out sprint with my legs tied and found I could come pretty close to my own best time in the one hundred as well.

But don't just take my word for it. Find the best swimmer in your pool, and do a little analytical work. Watch where your swimmer puts her hand on entry, check to see if she's using high elbow technique, watch where her hand comes out of the water, and, above all, try to see what the arm action is underwater where the power takes place. If you've picked out a really good swimmer, I'm sure you'll get the idea and become convinced as to the importance of arms in swimming.

Coaches will tell you that in the front crawl—the way most people swim—somewhere between 85 percent and 95 percent of all forward propulsion comes from the arms. That's pretty dramatic. I would modify the percentages a little. Sprinters going full tilt in a short race utilize an energy-burning big kick, and some of them actually do get up to 25 percent of their speed from their legs. But distance swimmers and serious, accomplished recreational swimmers will come in nearer the 9:1 ratio in favor of arms suggested at the beginning of this paragraph.

Feel for the Water

Effective arm action is clearly the important factor for good swimming. It's essential to understand how to develop it. One of the keys for proper arm action is something coaches refer to as "feel for the water." This is so critical to competent and enjoyable swimming that I've dedicated a short chapter on this subject a little later in this book. For now we will simply consider that feel for the water is a somewhat mysterious kinesthetic sense that provides neurological and muscular feedback to the swimmer that he or she utilizes automatically in making the most efficient stroking. Feel for the water is perhaps more than anything else what separates the good swimmers from the not so good. It's something that some develop more quickly than others.

Feel for the water is part relaxation, part kinesthetic sense and feedback, and part just blending with the water in a natural, comfortable way. Often, it can be developed over time as you become more used to swimming and the liquid environment it requires. While there are a lot of forces involved in completing each arm stroke, it's more important to develop a good measure of "feel" in the water than to understand the physics. You may wish to read the chapter on this subject that follows a little later in this book. Right now, however, it's time to analyze the mechanics of the arm action for crawl swimming.

The Process

The mechanics of any stroke can be seen as a logical process. When swimming the front crawl, each stroke begins with an entry in front of the shoulder; the lead arm then stretches forward and outward to a point where a "catch" is made where the hand's pressure on the water is felt. The catch can be looked upon as the point where the power phase of the stroke begins. This preliminary phase is followed by the "downsweep" where the action is primarily pulling through the water. The stroke then moves to a transition point where the arm, although bent at the elbow to some degree, is in a generally vertical position. This is followed by the "upsweep" to "release" where the hand leaves the water, hopefully well below the bottom of the bathing suit. This part of the stroke—the underwater action—which I refer to as the "power phase" should be long, so that the arm extends to its full length "to the release where the hand comes out of the water. The release takes place near midthigh. All of this is critical in accomplishing a long, efficient stroking action.

It's important to emphasize at this point the "high elbow" concept. In good swimming, the elbow stays higher than the hand from the catch to the finish. High elbows are key to avoiding a chronic stroke inefficiency seen in many lap swimmers: the "dropped" or "collapsed" elbow, a problem discussed later in this chapter.

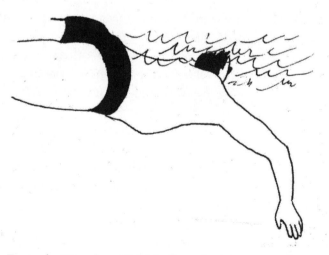

Freestyle. Note bent (high) elbow during arm stroke.

Coordination of both arms is essential, and the essence of coordination is timing. When you start one stroke—that is when you place one hand about shoulder width in the water in front of your head—your other arm should be just reaching the release point where it will leave the water. This is not a cut-and-dried part of the process because some swimmers utilize more "overlap" than others. Overlap is a concept involving stroke timing. There usually is a "resting" point during the "stretch" where you reach forward with your leading arm. A swimmer who uses a good deal of overlap in his or her stroking can be seen as almost waiting for each arm to catch up with the other before beginning the downsweep. The timing here is highly dependent upon feel for the water.

In good front crawl swimming, the arms work in several separate phases as I have described above. Coaches tend to describe the action individually and uniquely. Phil Whitten, for instance, in his fine book *The Complete Book of Swimming* writes entry, catch, pull, follow through, and recovery. That's a fairly simple description of the process. On the other hand, swimming guru Ernest Maglischo in *Swimming Faster*, now seen as a coach's bible for swimming, uses somewhat different terms. He describes the arm action phases as stretch, catch, downsweep, insweep, upsweep, and recovery. While the words used are different, both authors are talking about the same thing.

As you can see from the above, the front crawl arm stroke is not just the simple action of putting your hand in the water somewhere in front of your head and pulling backward. Some of the best descriptions of the arm stroke process can be found in Maglischo's book, *Swimming Faster*. This book goes into a great deal of detail. It's fairly technical since he has written primarily for a coaching audience, but for a full understanding of the sequential actions involved, it's well-worth reading. My comments are in bold italics.

a. *Entry. Enter your arm into the water directly in front of your shoulder with your elbow slightly flexed and your palm facing outward. (**Author's note: The most recent coaching now dispels the "palm facing outward" concept. It's an elegant way to swim, but it can cause shoulder problems.**)*

b. *Stretch. After entry, stretch your arm forward while the other arm completes its underwater stroke.*

c. *Catch. When that stroke is completed, press down and out on the water until you feel a solid catch. Your wrist should be flexed, and your palm should be pitched outward somewhat.*

d.   *Downsweep and insweep. Once the catch is made, sweep your hand downward and then inward toward the midline of your body. Slowly rotate your palm inward and upward as you do.*

e.   *Upsweep. When your hand passes your head, push the water out, up and back toward your thigh. Rotate your hand as you do so.*

f.   *Release. Release pressure on the water as your hand approaches your thigh. Then turn your palm inward so that your hand leaves the water on its side, little finger first.*

A Snapshot of the Process

Making sure that your stroke is long is critical. Many of the errors I see that lap swimmers make have a common thread—pulling out short! In fact, I've seen one or two hardworking swimmers who make their arm recovery so short that it's almost still in front of their shoulders. Do it that way, and you hardly have an arm stroke at all! Even pretty good competitive swimmers often have a less-extreme version of pulling short. And not only do short strokes fail to generate maximum efficiency, but they cause muscle tension and fatigue. The recommended long stroke is one of the critical factors that allow for a low stroke-per-pool-length count and efficient, fast swimming. One of the keys to a long stroke is making sure the hand exits the water midthigh, below the bottom of the suit. (There are a number of drills toward the end of this chapter, which will help to reinforce an efficient long stroke.)

Freestyle. Illustration shows nice high (flexed or bent) elbow recovery of right arm

Good swimmers seem to glide along almost effortlessly, but the effortless part is most definitely an illusion. They're working a lot harder than it looks, universally utilizing a long-stroking action. That means a good stretch out in front to the catch and then a solid long-stroking action underwater to the release point somewhere midthigh. There is an extended push underwater at this point in the stroke. A long stroke separates the highly competent from the just pretty good.

The Insweep and Elbows below the Water

The other aspect of the crawl arm action crucial to good swimming is the importance of the "insweep." This is where the elbow bend is critical. This bent elbow under the body is a terrific power generator. Some swimmers bend their elbows to almost ninety degrees. The point where the elbow bend is the greatest is at that arm position I have referred to as the "transition"—where the action changes from pulling to a pushing action. There are some finer points in all of this, involving sculling motions of the hands, but these really are more the province of our old friend feel for the water. As stated a little earlier in this chapter, feel for the water is so important that a whole chapter is devoted to that topic later in this book. It is sufficient for our present purposes to note that a significant elbow bend underwater of around twenty to forty-five degrees will help to provide a strong and longer arm stroke where the action takes place—underwater. Twenty to forty-five degrees or for some swimmers even more of an elbow bend is a fairly wide range to be sure, but the difference accommodates various body shapes, sizes, and strengths.

My first coach, Joe Watmough, used to say, "It doesn't matter what you're doing over the water, it's underwater that counts!" All true except that what we do above the water can lead to good or bad habits under the water where it truly does count. And the bent-elbow underwater is set up by the high elbow action in the recovery phase. This allows for better leverage—putting more in play the prime chest, back, and arm muscles, maximizing strength efficiency, and making it easier to position the hand to apply force most effectively.

Elbows above the Water: A Style that Leads to Efficiency

Despite Watmough's wisdom, what we do above the water with our arms can make a difference. The key is "high elbows." Each arm should bend at the elbow as you make the recovery over the water. As indicated above, maintaining high elbows during the over-the-water recovery phase sets up a proper high elbow (bent-arm action) under the water during the power phase of your stroke. The elbow should bend as the hand is lifted after finishing the stroke near the outside of the thigh. Then the elbow lifts, and in a very real way, you almost feel that your elbow is leading the recovery action.

Freestyle. Illustration shows the high elbow on recovery. As the left arm recovers the right is still extended but just beginning to stroke.

More on the Underwater Action

After the entry, the arm stretches and moves to the outside somewhat. Then shortly after the catch, the elbow flexes underwater as you press your hand down to set up a proper pulling or sweeping motion. An expert calls this "reaching around a very large barrel," but I usually say "reaching *over* a barrel." This position places your hand in a leading position at the beginning of the actual pull phase. The hand will reach a point where it and your arm (still flexed) are more or less pointing toward the bottom of the pool. This is the transition point where the muscular forces you exert change from a pulling motion to a pushing motion. Your hand will then continue to take the lead by pressing and sweeping backward to the release point. Another way of describing the proper high elbow stroking is some imagery supplied by *Good Swimming*'s technical advisor, Jane Berkman Brown, "The elbow stays higher than the hand from the catch to finish." The high elbow underwater will ensure that the elbow does not collapse or "drop."

Many lap swimmers suffer from dropped elbow. When we don't maintain high elbows, the result is loss of power. In fact, some swimmers actually drop or dip their elbows right after their hands enter the water. This unwanted motion becomes habitual when the swimmer does not utilize a "high elbow recovery." As a result, the hand twists in the water, which allows the little finger side of the hand to lead the hand incorrectly through the stroke. The hand then becomes more of a blade, slipping through the water. The result is a loss of power.

To demonstrate this for yourself, bend over slightly and reach out in front of you, keeping your arm straight. Your palm should be parallel to the floor. Now dip or drop your elbow. Note how your hand shifts so that the distal, little finger, side of the hand also drops. In the water, this would set up the unwanted slipping motion and result in a swimming stroke with very limited power. This poor technique underwater is often set up by poor technique in the recovery phase above the water. It is important to imagine the whole cycle and practice each part before putting it all together.

The Rolling Action

When you try this high elbow, long-stroking technique in the pool, you should remember that you should roll from side to side as you stroke. Reaching down or across your body with one arm should cause you to roll significantly in that direction, allowing the recovering arm on the opposite side to exit the water more easily. Then completing your stroke and moving to your opposite side, you will naturally roll toward that arm. This is expected and is encouraged. The rolling action, with both shoulders and hips properly coordinated, will enable you to develop full power from the longer muscles in your hips, chest, and back. It will also make breathing easier as you roll away from your breathing side, and your face and mouth more naturally come out of the water.

Hand Speed

Up to this point, nothing has been said about hand speed, something that is of special concern for racers. There is, of course, a correlation between hand speed (the pace that a swimmer moves his or her hand through the water while completing each stroke) and the speed at which the swimmer moves through the water. Top swimmers are said to be able to increase the speed of their hands from start to finish in each stroke. It is also likely that hand speed is a function of strength.

Good swimmers need to focus on maintaining a technically sound stroke, emphasizing stroke length and a low-stroke count rather than trying for hand speed.

As in all things, there's danger in fanaticism. Too much emphasis on hand speed usually results in a swimmer's "pulling out short" at the end of the stroke in an effort to gain forward momentum by faster stroking. Wrong! It just doesn't work that way. Long stroking is what we're working toward for good, efficient swimming. The other fault that often comes into play when hand speed is overemphasized is the dropped elbow. In an effort to increase hand speed and still maintain a long stroke, the swimmer will often inadvertently drop his elbow, losing power because his or her hand is now slipping through the water with the back edge of the palm leading. The stroke may be long but lacking in power.

The Arm Stroke Described as an *S*

As you can see in *Good Swimming*, the arm stroke is not just a simple circular motion from start to finish. The round 180-degree arc described by the arm strokes of swimmers in the earlier part of the twentieth century were not nearly as effective as today's lengthened "power-zone" stroking. The old-time stroke with its 180 degrees only provided forward power during the middle (bottom) third of the arc. That was the way swimmers did it a long time ago. But we know better now. A proper crawl swim stroke is often described today as an S stroke. The hand, underwater, follows the general outline of a figure S from beginning to finish. An extension in the horizontal front to back action keeps the arm and hand in the power zone for a greater period. Putting it another way, an extended power zone is created by the longer horizontal aspect of the modern stroke.

Drills

There are a number of drills you can use to help you refine your arm technique. Some of these allow you to focus on a single arm at a time. Others focus on the coordination of both arms at once. These are helpful drills; taken together, they provide key exercises that will help you imprint into your muscle/nervous system the arm motions required for good swimming. It is important to pay attention to shoulder-and-hip roll in all freestyle drills.

An important word of advice on drills: drills are exercises designed to help us make changes in the way we do our stroking, in other words, to help us "groove" muscular action in the water. They should be done slowly and deliberately. Rushing through drills at a fast pace often results in sloppy execution to the degree that the drills themselves do not accomplish their purpose of teaching good swimming.

Arms. Two opposite arm drills that allow you to fully concentrate on the motions of each arm are helpful. Both drills are similar. You swim using only one arm. In one of these drills, extend the nonswimming arm in front of you. In the other, keep the nonswimming arm at your side. In both exercises, swim a length of the pool and then switch arms. You should try to do two- or three-pool lengths with each arm. Think through the motion and arm action you're striving for—the S curve. Be sure to finish your stroke at midthigh.

Hands and arms. In this drill, you swim normally except that you drag the tips of your fingers along the surface of the water on the recovery, making sure to keep the recovering hand close to your body. To do this drill correctly, it is necessary to recover with a high elbow—the main point of the drill.

Coordination of strokes. Then there is the "catch-up" drill. One arm is out in front while the stroking arm completes the stroke and recovery. Only when the stroking hand enters the water do you begin your pull with your other arm. This drill is sometimes done by holding a stick in the extended hand. Before stroking with the other arm, the swimmer grasps the stick with the recovering hand. I'd recommend a couple of lengths of this daily if you're having trouble keeping your stroke long. Note that too much of this drill can teach "overlap swimming," which most good swimmers find awkward and tiring.

Fist swimming. Some coaches believe in "fist swimming." Make a fist and swim normally. This one can be helpful in developing feel for the water. Too much fist swimming can develop tension. I'd go easy on this drill.

Hand-and-finger tension. Learning swimmers often ask how tightly the fingers should be held together. The answer is "not rigidly tight." In fact, during the recovery phase, the hand should be quite relaxed. The thumb should be somewhat separate from the rest of the fingers during the underwater phase of the stroke although there may be a natural "coming together" of the thumb as the hand exits from the water. The relaxed finger position helps the swimmer gain feel for the water and helps stabilize the hand's action through the water during the pulling phases.

Paddles and buoy. I also recommend the use of a pull buoy and hand paddles to help you develop arm strength and feel for the water. A word of caution here. The extra resistance created by hand paddles can cause shoulder problems. If you're trying hand paddles for the first time, start with a small size and back off if things begin to hurt.

Pull buoys can be found in many pools. Hand paddles generally are harder to find. Any equipment you need can be purchased from a swim-supply house such as Arena, Finals, Kast-A-way, or Speedo. A full list with telephone numbers as well as other interesting information can be found in the appendix of *The Complete Book of Swimming*. The *Aquatic Directory* is also helpful. More on this in my chapter "Toys and Other Equipment" where I have furnished a list with telephone numbers.

In Short

To summarize, it's important to reemphasize the high elbow concept. High elbows and long strokes go together. Learning to pull energetically all the way through to below the bottom of your suit and gaining some mastery of the bent-elbow technique underwater while stroking are critical to good swimming. Just remember, the key truly is in your arms. And it's not that difficult, but it does take practice.

Chapter 5

The Flutter Kick for Freestyle

Good kicking is the pathway to good swimming. While the arms may provide significantly more forward propulsion in most strokes, the legs provide the base on which the swimmer builds his or her stroke.

I know a pretty good breaststroker. He has the most rigid ankles I've ever seen, but he swims butterfly and backstroke with his breaststroke frog kick, so his stiff ankles cost him only minimally. In college, he made honorable mention All American in his stroke specialty. Even so when he tries to do the freestyle flutter kick with a kickboard, he actually goes backward! His stiff ankles, ridged at a ninety-degree angle, somehow "pull" water in a reverse direction, causing him to go the wrong way.

But he's an exception. Most of us have considerably more flexibility in our ankles than my breaststroke friend. Accordingly, we can look forward to having more success when we do the freestyle (crawl) kick. We'll discuss ankle flexibility and relaxation further in this chapter, but the point here is to underscore that you can have pretty good success in this sport even if you have some physical limitations.

My first coach used to have a special trick for teaching beginners. Joe Watmough led Brown University's aquatic programs for more than twenty-two years. Back in the 1950s and 1960s, each student had to pass a basic swim test. Joe was supposed to teach those who were unable to pass, but he didn't have a great deal of extra time for these students. To get them started, he gave each a kickboard and explained how the legs were supposed to work in the water. "Up and down, a little bend at the knee on the downstroke with a straightening of the leg on the up cycle and nice and relaxed at the ankles," he'd say, "that's it!" He'd shout from the pool edge, "You're doing the flutter kick!"

The boards were huge. You could almost lie on them and go to sleep when you did your kicking. Back in those days—not unlike today—the kick was seen as the building block upon which the rest of the stroke would grow. So Joe's nonswimmers would push off from the wall and kick across the pool repeatedly, time after time.

The theory, though simple, was sound. Most of these students eventually learned to swim at least well enough to pass the mandatory test required for graduation. The kicking exercise accomplished two goals. First, these neophyte swimmers learned something about the importance of keeping the body prone in the water. Second, they learned how their legs were supposed to work so that once they started actual swimming, adding arms to the stroke, their legs would kick almost automatically. And that's important; with so many new things to think about when you first learn to swim, it's very important when part of it is automatic.

Do the Legs Actually Provide Propulsion?

For most lap swimmers, the role for the kick is mostly to generate enough momentum to keep their legs somewhere near the surface, thus maintaining a good prone position in the water. Research has been conducted to determine exactly how much, if any, forward propulsion is exerted in the flutter kick and how much energy is expended in the process. The experiments, featuring topnotch, competitive swimmers, did show that the legs provided definite forward momentum to the stroke, but at an exorbitant cost in energy compared to the production and return on energy for arm stroking.

Unfortunately, most of the workout swimmers I see tend to swim relying on too much kicking and not enough arm action. One of the outcomes of this is actually getting less exercise. We think of swimming as a sport where the entire body is exercised. True, but only with good swimming. The typical lap swimmer who emphasizes his kick usually kicks slowly and deliberately. Often, his arms provide little propulsion while most of his energy is devoted to kicking. By slowing things down to accommodate the tempo of their kicking, many of these swimmers shortchange their arms. And since their entire mechanical systems are running on "slow," they shortchange the heart as well.

For most lap swimmers, the high-energy cost of kicking means there is less energy available for the arms. Further, too vigorous a kick will throw the rhythm of the arms and hands off. The result of all this is slower, less elegant, less comfortable swimming.

Most lap swimmers seek to achieve a maximum workout, something that can best be accomplished through good swimming, utilizing the most efficient mechanics possible. When the athlete swims inefficiently, different aspects of the body are not exercised to the full degree. When a swimmer moves his legs slowly and allows his arms to "drift," the net result is generally a complete slow down resulting in a not-so-good cardiovascular workout. With good swimming, the swimmer moves faster and more comfortably in the water, exercising harder but with seemingly less effort, and thus achieves a much better and more enjoyable cardiovascular workout. He or she also looks a lot better in the water. It's just a whole lot more fun doing it right!

The Legs Seen as Stabilizers That Keep the Swimmer Prone

We definitely need to be able to count on enough action from our legs to keep us in a nice, prone position in the water. Otherwise, our legs will drop, leading to a head-up-feet-down position in the water that creates far too much drag for good swimming. Relaxation is important in accomplishing a proper, level position in the water, something that is critically important in good swimming. Skillful swimmers invariably prone out in the water nicely. And they do it with a relaxed style.

In the crawl's traditional six-beat flutter kick, the big muscles of the back and stomach come into play while the knee and everything below should be relaxed, just going along for the ride provided by the thigh. The big muscles power the thigh up and down and act as stabilizers, subtly keeping the swimmer in sync with the water while setting up the quads and hamstrings to provide force for the kick. As for the kick, it's like a whip. The thigh is the handle of the whip, and the lower leg and foot are at the far end where the snap takes place. The snap provides an extra boost of propulsion.

The Whip Action Versus Straight Legs

Were you taught to keep your legs absolutely straight when you swim? That bit of bad teaching put many of us on the wrong track. There's a good deal of leg bend in an efficient, modern flutter kick. Visualize yourself as lying in the water, facedown. Press one of your thighs toward the bottom of the pool. At this point, *assuming you're keeping the lower leg properly relaxed,* your knee will bend due to water resistance. The knee should bend to form an angle of about thirty to thirty-five degrees. Your knee will drop about eight inches to a foot toward the pool bottom; then you will—using the muscles on the dorsal (rear) side of your thigh and lower back—cause your thigh to change direction, lifting and sending the back of the knee toward the surface of the water.

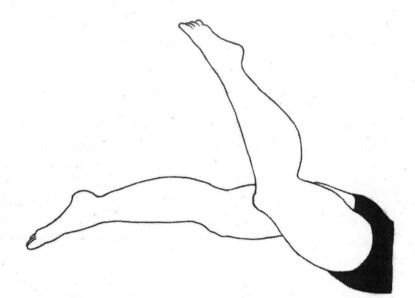

Freestyle. Flutter kick with right leg starting downward path, knee beginning its bend, left leg starting an upward path

This change of direction is the point where the "snapping of a whip" analogy comes alive. As your thigh and the back of your knee begin to track toward the surface, your lower leg and foot will continue for an instant toward the pool bottom before the new direction change catches up with this more distant part of your leg. The upward motion of the thigh should involve substantial energy and the lower part of your leg—everything including and below the knee—should be relaxed. Ankle relaxation is particularly important. Without relaxation, there is no "snap" and far less propulsion.

As this upward action of the thigh continues, your leg will straighten of its own accord. Assuming you're nicely relaxed, the pressure of the water against your lower leg will cause this straightening rather than any voluntary mechanical force you exert. Your leg, now straightened, continues on an upward path until your foot is at or just below the surface of the water. Then the sequence begins again with another snap of the whip as your leg moves down in the water.

The Stealth Kick

It's generally thought that the feet should not come out of the water. To quote the popular coach Terry Laughlin, "A splashy kicker is kicking air half the time, and air will get you nowhere." The fix is the "stealth" kick—no noise, no splash. Yet some excellent swimmers—usually sprinters—do raise their feet above the surface when kicking. This is a function of an especially vigorous kick, and the downward action of the feet in such swimmers seems to provide an element of lift in their chests and shoulders.

Having a better understanding of the correct mechanics required in the flutter kick, one can well understand how the bad instruction of "keep those legs straight!" originated. The legs should be straight but only for the upbeat part of the leg action. Keeping them straight throughout the entire kick requires a rigid and incorrect application of muscular force, not consistent with the relaxation required in efficient kicking. That's just one of the interesting idiosyncrasies we find so often in swimming—the need to apply muscular force in a relaxed manner.

Relaxation Is Key

So a relaxed, flexible ankle and foot are particularly important to good swimming. Most competitive freestylers, butterflyers, and backstrokers have very flexible ankles. This flexibility allows the swimmer's ankles to bend and act like small flippers, providing a measure of propulsion. Stiff ankles can be the death knell to a good kick. This flexibility or lack of it is to a large degree a characteristic we are born with. There are stretching exercises that can increase ankle flexibility to some degree by increasing range of motion. For instance, sitting in a chair, you bend one leg underneath of your seat, top of your foot down with your toes on the floor. Simply press down with your leg to feel the stretching action. You can stretch the other way by standing and, keeping your feet flat on the floor, bend forward as far as you can. A good range of motion here will allow you to press your knees several inches ahead of your toes.

There are three factors involved here: range of motion, flexibility, and the ability to relax your ankles while kicking to allow the first two aspects—range of motion and flexibility to come into play. The best approach when working on your kick is to utilize the kickboard and think about using a fairly deep kick, stretching your range of motion a little, keeping in mind relaxed ankles and overall flexibility in your legs. Be sure to remember to bend at the knees on the down thrust. The mind-set should be flexibility and relaxation as you kick that board along in the water.

For Chronically Stiff Ankles, Go with the Flow

But even if you have truly stiff ankles, all is not lost. Like the vignette at the beginning of this chapter about my friend who was an All American in college in his breaststroke specialty, there are many pretty darn good swimmers around enjoying their swimming and even competing in various events in Masters meets who have the stiff ankle problem. My advice to these folks is to really work on their arms. If stiff ankles are your nemesis, learn to swim off your arms. Back off the legs as much as you can, expend as little energy as possible on leg action. Use your legs only enough to provide stability. Do not expect forward propulsion. That's what you've got arms for.

Variations in Kicking Rhythms

Kicking is like putting on our pants; we do it one leg at a time. Even so, a definite rhythmic action is required. One leg goes down while the other goes up, working in opposition. For some reason, a "six-beat" action seems to be the most natural. Six beats means that for each complete arm cycle (left and right), there are six leg kicks (three on each side). In other words, a six-beat kick means each leg will kick three times while each arm is stroking once.

I go into more detail about coordinating the arms and legs in the chapter titled "Bringing It All Together," but for now, we'll stick to the kick itself. There are other kicking rhythms—the two-beat kick and the four-beat kick. The two-beat style is especially good for distance freestylers as it is an energy saver. The kick is two kicks (one left and one right) for each arm cycle. Again, it's one kick on each side for each arm stroke. The kicking rhythm for the two beat is much slower and more deliberate than the rhythm required for the six beat. A down thrust of the leg is applied toward the end of the pulling cycle for the arm on the same side. One of the benefits of the two-beat kick is that it encourages proper hip rotation, which in turn transfers more power to the arms. The four-beat kick is more unusual, and swimmers who utilize it generally execute four fairly strong kicks plus some other, often rather bizarre leg movements, making it more of a modified six-beat kick.

Making It Natural and Relaxed

Just like my old coach, I generally advise new swimmers to learn to kick using a kickboard. The idea is to get the mechanics ingrained into your system so you won't have to think about them. Then when you turn to actual swimming, you can concentrate on your arms, moving them through the water in the correct pattern forcefully so that they take the lead in your swimming. If you do it this way and have done some work with the kickboard, your legs are sure to make reasonably efficient movements in the water, which will keep them somewhere near the surface, allowing you to maintain a prone position.

Another tip—when you're working on your kick, it's important to emphasize the up action of each leg. The down action, where the knee will bend to some degree, is more natural. Getting your legs to work with a forceful snap that will allow the whip-cracking action takes a little more effort and emphasis on the up movement. The up action should be a natural reaction to the downbeat. Emphasizing a strong extensive action immediately after the downbeat will help provide a stronger upbeat.

And above all, stay relaxed.

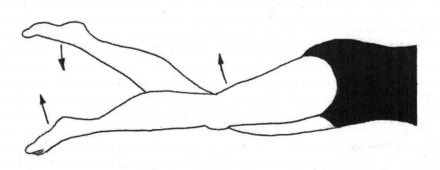

Freestyle. Illustration shows another view of the flutter kick. Arrows indicate pathway of each leg

It's a paradox, but you have to put out a fair amount of effort—muscle power—in swimming, but at the same time, you must be relaxed. Relaxation, like all the rest, is something that must be learned. That's one of the reasons I recommend isolating your attention as much as possible on each new movement while you learn, committing the new skill to the reflex system so that the higher, thinking brain won't have to deal with it later when you're putting everything together for regular swimming. Concentrating on too many physical activities at the same time causes "overload" and muscular tension. That's why I recommend using hand paddles and a pull buoy to isolate your arm action and why I recommend using a kickboard. I use both every day.

Drills and Tips

Still, remembering Coach Laughlin's tip about the "stealth" kick—the kind of kick most lap swimmers need, keeping your feet just under the surface to avoid the "air" kicking, I recommend a drill utilized by Coach Dan Patton. The drill emphasizes body and hip roll, which are important to good swimming. Patton calls the drill the "six- or twelve-kick switch." It's simple. The swimmer kicks on her side with the lower arm outstretched directly ahead and the top arm on the hip. After six or twelve kicks, change sides by doing a good freestyle pull. While this drill is directed more to teaching the critical body-roll concept, it also teaches us that a kickboard is not always necessary.

To avoid air kicking, I also recommend that you do *some* of your regular kicking with no board. When doing this, remember to breathe during a regular six-beat sequence. The best way is to roll your head to your breathing side and take a quick breath, then exhale completely during the six-beat cycle with your head in a normal swimming position as you kick.

This chapter has covered freestyle or front-crawl kicking. The kicking action in front crawl, backstroke (back crawl), and butterfly are all quite similar. In backstroke, the kick is identical except that the swimmer is on his back, and therefore, all the leg motions are the same except inverted. The butterfly kick can be seen as the same as freestyle except you kick with both legs at the same time. Actually, you have to put a little more back action (undulation) into it. Jane Berkman Brown, one of the technical advisors for *Good Swimming*, describes the butterfly kick as "popping the hips much more than with other strokes." True, but even with the butterfly, we're essentially using the same muscle groups in pretty much the same way they are used for front crawl.

So the final tip in this chapter is to emulate my old coach and get out the kickboard. And practice, practice, practice until you get the kick down to the point that it's a natural, repeating action you don't have to think about. This natural, repeating kick will happen a lot quicker than you may think, but you've got to work at it.

Chapter 6

Bringing It All Together:
Breathing, Arms, and Kick

This chapter for the most part is geared to the needs of the neophyte although there are tips helpful to most lap swimmers. Competitors and upper-echelon lap swimmers should be beyond most of this material although even better swimmers might take note of the ten common errors at the chapter's end.

Joan is one of the early bird swimmers at the pool where I work out. Lately, I've been working with her stroke and emphasizing relaxation. One of her issues had been lazy arms. Her tendency was to pull out a little short and not finish her stroke. After working with her for a while, she managed to change to longer stroking, but she still had very little "push" where it's especially important, late in the stroke just before the hands exit the water. We got that corrected all right, but I noticed she had a serious relaxation problem. She looked a lot better in the water technically, but you could tell her muscles were very tight.

The next step was my favorite drill: finger dragging. This drill is described in the book's earlier chapter, *"The Key Is in Your Arms."* As this is written, Joan is looking a whole lot better, at least when she does the drill. The relaxation is coming.

The point here is to emphasize the importance of relaxation in good swimming. I've seen thousands of excellent swimmers over the years, and without exception, one quality they all share is the ability to put out a lot of energy and muscle power and, at the same time, stay very relaxed. This sounds like a paradox, but it's very true. It can be a lot to ask, but the ability to perform in a relaxed way is something seen in many, probably most, and perhaps all athletic endeavors. And it's something to keep in mind as you move to the next step in your quest to good swimming.

You should be ready now for the next step in good swimming: putting it all together. You've worked on your breathing to the point you're pretty comfortable in the water and can take those hundred breaths without panting or becoming breathless, you've worked out most of the obvious kinks in your arm action and have done a good deal of swimming with the pull buoy, you've got a pretty good understanding and feel for a level, prone position in the water, and you've tortured yourself with the kickboard so that now your kick is beginning to feel natural. Having done all this, you're definitely ready. In fact, you may be a little ahead of the game.

Your work with the pull buoy came pretty close to actually swimming, and you had to control any breathing problems you may have had in order to make forward progress. It's a lot simpler to get your breathing problems under control when you're just swimming with your arms. Pulling with a buoy uses a smaller amount of energy and doesn't require as much oxygen. Using less oxygen means needing less air and easier breath control.

No-Breath Swimming (A Learning Shortcut)

There's one other step that can be helpful as we try to bring things together in a coordinated fashion. I hesitate to bring it up because breathing is so essential; still, many people find it useful to forget breathing for a few moments as they concentrate on coordinating the other two important skills—arm action and kicking. It's done this way: in the shallow end of the pool, push off with your face in the water and start swimming using both your arms and legs. Forget the breathing for now. Just keep your face in the water. Concentrate on a full, active arm motion and make your legs work just the way they've been doing with the kickboard. Let your breath out slowly, but don't try to take in air. Swim this way, your face down in the water for just a few strokes.

Take five or ten of these short bursts of swimming. Certainly, you won't go very far without fresh air, but you'll be able to focus on the coordination of both your arms and legs. Be sure to concentrate on making nice long arm strokes. Try to stay relaxed. Usually, people are quite amazed at how strongly they're able to stroke. Suddenly, they feel like accomplished swimmers. This is a marvelous way to get the feel for moving correctly in the water.

On the other hand, this is something you may be able to skip if you've been successful with the pull buoy, stroking either with or without hand paddles. Still, many folks find that they need this step even after they've become proficient pullers. It comes down to that all-important beginning—learning to breathe comfortably while in the sometimes unfriendly environment of water.

Timing for Air

The coordination of breathing and stroking is fairly simple. You should turn your head to take that bite of air just as your breathing side arm comes out of the water to begin its recovery. This means that you will be looking under your recovering arm as you breathe. You only have a split second to take in air, so you have to remember to prepare by emptying your lungs—blowing it all out—when your face is in the water. Then you'll be ready to inhale when that arm begins its recovery cycle.

Only one eye should be out of the water at the point of breathing. We often see swimmers who turn their heads too far and seem to look at the ceiling when they breathe. The result of this error of turning the head too far usually means turning the shoulder too far with awkward, nonrelaxed swimming. In addition, you should look slightly ahead when breathing in order to keep your head and body in the optimal position.

Head Position

The position of your head is important. Assuming you're getting enough out of your kick to keep your legs and feet somewhere near the surface, adjustments in your body position can be made based on how deep or how shallow you hold your head in the water. The rule is simple: your body will follow the lead of your head. And you want to keep your body moving in one line without a lot of unnecessary wiggling.

Most of us like to have the waterline on our heads beginning just above the eyebrows and running to the back of the head carrying along just above our ears. At least, that's the way I learned it. Today, swimmers are taught to look more toward the bottom of the pool, which in turn will bring the waterline a little higher on the forehead. Even so today in the front crawl, most swimmers look somewhat forward toward the end of the pool rather than directly at the bottom. The exact head position will vary from swimmer to swimmer depending upon body shape and physical make up. A person with heavy legs that tend to sink will be more likely to carry his head lower in the water and to look more toward the bottom to counterbalance the sinking action of the legs. A person with lighter legs will generally swim with her head in a higher position. But most of us will find the most comfortable and productive waterline to be somewhat above the eyebrows.

Stroke Count

Alexander Popov, a Russian who—around the turn of the twenty-first century was acclaimed the world's fastest swimmer—swam and trained differently than other elite swimmers, including Americans as well as athletes from elsewhere in the world. Not only did he carry his head lower, but also, he put great emphasis on a low stroke count. This means that Popov spent considerable training time working on stroke efficiency—*going the greatest distance in the fewest number of strokes.*

Coaches track the number of strokes required by swimmers to swim a length of the pool. A tall man with long arms, Popov required only thirty-three strokes for fifty meters in winning his first gold medal at the 1992 Barcelona Olympics. (Each hand entry is counted as a stroke.) Popov trains at slow speeds working on mechanics, relaxation, and pulling length. In training sessions, his stroke count can go as low as twenty-five per fifty meters. In a twenty-five-yard pool, this would equal an incredible eight strokes per length. (How does this compare with your own stroke count? A competent workout swimmer will do around twenty strokes per twenty-five yards.) Popov's secret was a happy combination of size, strength, long arms, relaxation, a strong kick, and marvelous stroke mechanics.

In an article published in the February 1999 *Lane Line,* the Delaware Valley Masters Swimming Committee newsletter, Coach Terry Laughlin writes, "The current holder of the title 'World's Fastest Human' traveled a distinctly different path to his dominance in freestyle sprinting, one that fitness swimmers should find far more inviting and practical to emulate than the more conventional route of pain, torture, and agony."

In citing "pain, torture, and agony," Laughlin is referring to the more accepted training regimens world-class swimmers submit to, which generally include daily yardages in the twelve thousand to eighteen thousand and up ranges. This is ten miles or so of swimming daily spread over two or even three sessions that consist of an eclectic variety of drills and gut-wrenching swims, many of which are completed at high speed.

Laughlin suggests that most of us would benefit by emulating Popov. In other words, swim slower but make every stroke count. Work on efficiency. *Stay relaxed.* Try to become more streamlined in the water, maintaining a long axis, thinking of your arms and hands as extensions of your body to add length. He suggests looking at the bottom of the pool to keep your head lower so that just a small part of the back of your head shows above water. And he strongly emphasizes the need to keep each stroke long.

Despite the fact that this method works for Popov, I'm a little skeptical. Popov is a unique swimming talent. He's also a sprinter, something most fitness swimmers are not. Would the same kind of training regimen, with its shorter daily yardage and extreme emphasis on technique, work universally for all of us? Perhaps, but who knows at this point? We're just not seeing a lot of other swimmers training Popov's way.

And then Matt Kredich, head coach for women at The University of Tennessee and a technical advisor for this book, notes that Popov does indeed pick his yardage up to the one-hundred-thousand-per-week category for a couple of weeks just prior to his taper period when preparing for an especially big meet, such as the Olympics. Kredich also notes that during this period, about 20 percent of Popov's training is of the high-stress variety, and that his regular daily regimen calls for at least one all-out fifty-meter sprint. So Popov may be more in line with how most swimmers train than what some of us would think.

As for daily yardage, even when not in the final pretaper training weeks for a big meet, Popov goes at least four times as far as even the more ambitious lap swimmers. So I'm certainly not recommending any of us reduce our daily yardage. Further, fitness swimming equates more generally to distance swimming than to sprinting. That means the training must be different. On the other hand, there is much to be learned from the emphasis on technique, keeping the stroke long, counting your strokes in the pool, trying to stay relaxed, trying to keep your body long in the water, and perhaps even giving the lower head position a shot.

The Rolling Action

One of the routes to gaining a longer stroke is learning to roll properly. We've already indicated that some body roll is desirable. Our bodies should roll toward the arm doing the stroking. This will allow for a stronger, more efficient pull and will facilitate breathing when we roll away from the breathing side allowing our mouths to take in air more easily. The roll is begun right after the hand enters the water, during the stretch/catch phase of stroking, just before the downsweep begins. When done correctly, you will feel a slight muscle tension in the pectoral muscles of the upper chest just as you begin to roll to that side.

The concept of body roll in the freestyle is a fairly recent development. In my college days, the emphasis was on the driving kick and maintaining a high head, high chest, flat, prone body position. This was the Johnny Weissmuller style, obviously very successful in its day. Swimming this way demanded a terrific kicking action, and modern research has shown this older method to be less effective than a rolling style of swimming.

It's a good idea when working on the rolling action to practice alternate breathing—breathing on both sides while skipping a breath in the middle. This will help you balance your stroke so that you don't end with a pronounced roll on your breathing side while staying fairly flat on your nonbreathing side.

Front crawl, along with backstroke, are considered "long axis" strokes. What this means is that the muscular force is developed along a longer aspect of the body than in the short axis strokes—butterfly and breaststroke. A correct body roll, which includes both shoulders and hips, just prior to applying the muscular activity for the stroke, enables us to put in play more efficiently the body's long muscles of the back and chest. These are some of the strongest muscles in our bodies, and much of the muscular drive for swimming in front crawl and backstroke actually begins from the hips. With this in mind, it is understandable that using your arms in swimming is a great deal more than just putting your hand in the water and pulling back.

Compromises

But don't get carried away with all the emphasis on shoulder roll, upper-body roll, and even hip roll. Coaches will argue how much of each is correct for each of their swimmers. I've seen some wonderful swimmers who swam absolutely flat in the water. It can be done, and many folks feel good doing it that way. Depending upon how long you've been swimming, your age, and perhaps most important, what your objectives are, you can decide for yourself how far you want to go along the road to picture-book swimming. Whatever your goals are, you do need to remember that your arms are critically important. They should be the driving force that leads you forward—not your legs. Getting it right with your arms and your breathing will enable you to be a first-rate swimmer even when your legs do little or nothing for you.

A Recap

Putting it all together starts with head position. That will set up your body position and breathing mechanics, and to a degree dictate the amount of body roll you'll need, at least on your breathing side. Body roll should, of course, be kept fairly equal on both sides. A nice, prone body position in the water will make good arm mechanics flow more easily. Strong arm action will then move you along at a better pace, allowing the legs to rise more naturally toward the surface, utilizing the minimal kicking action I advise for most lap swimmers.

That's really it in a nutshell. You won't be swimming like Alexander Popov or Michael Phelps, but you will be swimming a lot better, moving with an efficiency you have not had before. Your breathing will be natural, and your need for air determined solely by the energy you're expending and your speed in the water. It will be a truly wonderful feeling. You'll be keeping those strokes long and efficient, flowing with the water in a strong but seemingly effortless, relaxed way.

That flowing effortlessness we see in good swimmers is something of an illusion. It may look effortless, but there is considerable power and effort being applied. This is the signature of a good swimmer: the ability to apply force with grace (relaxation) and efficiency. We see this in other sports, and it should be our aim to develop as much of it as we can. In swimming, the key is in the relaxed way we expend our energy, seeking stroke length, not fighting the water, but blending and seeking to become one with it.

About Stroking Errors

There are a number of common errors I see in lap swimmers. Generally, these are correctable, and correcting them will lead to better and more comfortable swimming. Of course, the problem with old mechanical aberrations ingrained into our nerve and musculature systems is that they can only be corrected with hard work. And as we make adjustments toward more ideal mechanics, we usually find these changes initially uncomfortable. This is expected, and it is critically important to press ahead with our corrections. Eventually, they will feel more natural, but our old habits do not die easily.

At one of the pools where I train, I have a friend who swims about a mile a day. His swimming is painful for me to watch. He has a number of peculiarities in his arm stroke and breathing that creates a great deal of drag. Because his mechanics are so poor, he spends a long time in the pool swimming slowly. I offered him some help one day. I suggested a more elevated head position and showed him a more normal and longer arm pull. He was beginning to look a lot better in the water, and he was moving faster without putting out more effort.

But the changes didn't feel comfortable to him. This is the common phenomenon with people who have been doing things the wrong way for a long time. The problem is, the wrong way feels right! This creates a psychological barrier that must be overcome if progress is to be made. My friend told me he was going to keep working at it, but it hasn't happened. The desire for better swimming just isn't there, and consequently for him, the extra work and concentration on doing his swimming correctly just isn't worth it. One thing I'll give him—he does get a good work out doing it his way. He's not pretty in the water, but he's using lots of energy.

Ten Common Errors

Not expelling a full breath underwater. This mistake can cause lots of problems when the swimmer holds his breath too long. In order for your lungs to be ready to accept more air, you have to get rid of the last breath you took. So before you turn your head for the next breath, you should expel the last one underwater. Some swimmers have the habit of holding their breath or at least partially holding it. The result is a carbon dioxide buildup and breathlessness. The cure is concentration on getting rid of all your air while your head is underwater prior to turning to get a breath.

Raising the head to breathe. This one comes in lots of forms. Some folks lift their heads forward; others do it with more of a swivel action following the movement of the recovering arm. For every action, there is an equal and opposite reaction. When the head is raised, the body is lowered, particularly the legs, creating extra drag. To correct this flaw, it is important to learn to roll properly, coordinating a simple head-turning action at the neck. The reality is that your mouth does not have to be above the waterline for you to catch a bite of air. When you turn your head, an air pocket will form around your mouth. This and all turning actions should be along the longitudinal axis of your body in freestyle. Anything else is disruptive.

A short arm pull. Beginners and experts alike can suffer from this flaw. I've seen lap swimmers who are so short with their arms that their pull is little more than a dog paddle. At the competitive level, particularly when we move to a full sprint, swimmers have a tendency to cut their strokes off with an early recovery, seeking to speed up by stroking faster. The shortened stroke means that actually, we swim slower and use more energy doing it. The answer is to always keep the stroke count as low as possible. Here's where we should emulate Popov. Count your strokes. You won't get it down to eight per pool length, but you can find your own improvement level. Remember, your hand should press back in the water well below your hips.

A bouncing stroke. This can occur if a swimmer presses down on the water prematurely without the good hand-and-arm extension that would lead to correct underwater stroke mechanics. The cure is utilization of greater forward reach in the stroke by the swimmer.

Lazy arms. This is seen usually in conjunction with overkicking. The swimmer tends to move slowly in the water relying on the kick for forward propulsion at the same time letting her arms drift in the water rather than exerting a strong pulling action. The cure is emphasis on the long pull, correct mechanics underwater, and practice with the pull buoy.

The fish tail wiggle. This is caused by improper arm recovery sometimes compounded by lifting the head to breathe. The cure is to learn to make the proper longitudinal body turn to each side as you stroke. Most wigglers are using their arms, perhaps not to optimal efficiency, but at least to the degree that they are producing forward momentum. Again, the cure is learning to roll correctly and finding the correct entry point for the hand on recovery and then making the proper stretch and catch, forward and not across the midline in front of the head. Alternate-side breathing can help.

The dropped elbow. This has been mentioned before. It's a classic and something seen in even good, competitive swimmers. The dropped elbow occurs right after the hand enters the water. Some people seem to rotate their hands on entry so that their palms face the head. This rotation can cause the elbow to drop and sets the arm up for a weak pull, lacking good water contact. The dropped elbow can also occur without hand rotation. The cure is to use a high elbow recovery, making sure that your hand enters the water either flat or with the palm facing slightly outward. This will set your hand and arm up for a strong stretch, catch, and pull. Remember the feeling that you're reaching over a barrel as you start your pull. But a note of caution here: too much thumb-first hand entry can result in shoulder problems. Find the happy medium, remembering that the high elbow is critically important.

The wandering kick. Some swimmers use what almost appears to be a sidestroke kick when they roll to breathe. The old Red Cross handbook refers to this as a trudgen crawl. It's slower, but it does work; however, it can be a little dangerous to other swimmers in the same or even nearby lanes. I've been kicked rather painfully by swimmers using this style. It's a relatively inefficient way to swim. The cure is to do more kicking with the kickboard to groove your flutter kick to the point where it is totally natural for you. Breathing errors involving too much body roll can result in a "wandering kick." Using the correct amount of roll will lessen the invitation to your body to make this unwanted move.

Carrying the head too low. Some swimmers actually bury their heads in the water when they swim, throwing their body position out of alignment. This position usually results in the swimmer's hips being carried too high for good control. Also, breathing from the low-head position is difficult and usually will involve lifting the head. As usual, one error can set up a sequence of other errors that create drag and other inefficiencies. The cure is to do some head-up swimming—actual swimming with your head out of the water, looking directly ahead, then dropping to a head position where the waterline is just above the goggles. The habit of carrying your head too low can be one of the more difficult flaws to cure because after months and years of swimming this way, it has become comfortable despite its inefficiency. Like most bad habits, it can be cured but only with hard work and patience.

Slapping the hands into the water on entry. This habit can be the result of trying to recover too fast with your arms. Usually, it occurs when a swimmer tries to speed up. This is another of those quirks that make us inefficient as we swim. The cure is to stay relaxed, slow the recovery down, and remember to keep your stroke long.

I've pointed out ten errors. There are many other things swimmers do incorrectly, but these ten are often seen in lap swimmers of varying abilities. Interestingly, many of them have something to do with improper arm action. Again, we see the emphasis on good arm stroking as being the critical ingredient leading to efficient swimming. The other common denominator in these errors has to do with body position. For good swimming, it's critical to maintain a level position in the water.

In Conclusion

Putting it all together isn't necessarily easy. For some folks, it just happens naturally. Others have to work at it with intense concentration. I wrote a lot about imaging in the third chapter. Imaging can help greatly as you try to master this first step in crawl swimming. You'll be able to pattern your moves on those of some excellent aquatic practitioners when they are pointed out to you. I can guarantee you'll get a lot of satisfaction when you notice bad habits being replaced by good ones as you follow your quest to good swimming.

Chapter 7

Developing a Feel for the Water

This is an important chapter for those seeking improvements in their swimming. Feel for the water can often be overlooked, particularly for those who are primarily self-coached.

Coaches talk about it all the time, "Swimmer X has great feel for the water!" or "Swimmer Y needs to develop a better feel for the water." It sounds mystical and mysterious, but it's reality.

Feel for the water is swimming's version of something that goes on in all sports—kinesthetic feedback, the ability to feel your way through what you're doing, and then make the necessary adjustments to do it better. The difference between what happens in swimming may well be that you have a near-naked body totally immersed in a liquid medium through which it is supposed to travel so that the opportunity is greater, and the necessity for developing this feel even more essential than in other sports.

John Jerome in his book, *Staying with It*, has an interesting comment on this kinesthetic sense:

> *The kinesthetic sense is what teaches the skier to ride on a flat ski, the racing driver to learn that smoother is, finally, faster. It is the capacity to sense the forces that will be needed and to marshal them; to perceive the forces at work and to cut through them to the quickest, cleanest way. As with the Taoist cook asked why his knife never needs sharpening; simple, he says, he doesn't cut the meat, he just uses his knife to separate it, following the natural divisions of the flesh.*

I'm not sure that any of us know exactly how this kinesthetic sense works. Even so, the feelings we get from any sport are part of that sport's special joy: the solid click of a sharply hit golf ball, the feel of a well-struck tennis ball, the flow of nicely linked turns on a steep ski slope, the rush and sudden lift when a surfer picks up a wave, and then of course, there's the thrill of the ride itself.

The biofeedback mechanism in swimming may well be unique or at least go beyond what we find in other activities less dependent upon our involvement in the medium. Swim coaches understanding this, work with their athletes to heighten their awareness for this feel for the water.

A Special Tip for Triathletes and Other Competitors: The Shave

Before important meets, coaches have their swimmers "shave down." This involves a total body shave with some especially dedicated athletes even shaving their heads. Shaving does at least three things to improve swimming performances. Taking off body hair reduces drag; swimmers with the most body hair universally will get the most benefit from the shave. Then there is the placebo effect; the athlete thinks the shave will help, and therefore it does. One theory holds that shaving somehow makes the nerve ending receptors in the skin more sensitive to the various pressures and sensations of the water, thus heightening the body's own feedback mechanism. This sounds reasonable although others argue that shaving masks the nerve receptors. In swimming as in advanced physics, the realm of the theory can be confusing. The whys and whyfors are less important than the knowledge that it works.

The sensations of swimming when you are newly shaved include a greatly heightened awareness. You seem to slip easily through the water, stronger and more capable. Your body somehow seems to know more clearly what to do. You're in tune with your liquid environment, and you're in your own special world where you are queen or king. It is a wonderful feeling—a byproduct of a ritual practice for speed—a confidence builder for the coming competition.

But obviously, competitors can't body shave every day. In fact, if we tried, it wouldn't work. Any placebo effect would wear off with the reality of an everyday body shave, and in all probability, the nerve receptors in our skin also would desensitize. It follows that the effect of the swimmer's shave is short lived, and coaches generally feel that shaving is only effective if done no more than three times a year. Shaving, however, is just one—albeit very special—technique for increasing a swimmer's feel for the water.

Sculling

One of the most important coaching tricks for developing feel for the water is sculling. There are several ways to do a sculling drill: on your stomach; side; back, hands in front, hands at your sides; or, while vertically, in the water. Sculling is a drill where you work your hands and arms in the water, drawing them back and forth, changing the attack angle of your hands so that you feel the water and feel the various propulsive forces involved as you move your hands in this exercise. Rowdy Gaines, once one of the country's premier sprinters, and now a coach and sometime Masters swimmer, had some comments about feeling the water and sculling in an April 1991 article in *Swim* (a now defunct magazine directed to Masters swimmers):

> *Learn to feel the water. Be one with the water. Don't fight against the water. From your fingertips to your elbow is where you do a lot of work in freestyle, so do a lot of sculling drills to help that feel.*

I'd argue that from the fingertips to the elbow is where you do a lot of work in all styles of swimming. In all the strokes, the end result of force action happens from the elbows to the fingertips. Otherwise, Gaines' comments are useful. Gaines goes on to tell us to do what comes naturally, not to think too much about what we're trying to do and to relax in the water. How right he is!

More on Imaging

Imaging is another technique that can help us gain feel for the water. When I'm about to compete in the butterfly, I usually imagine how my race will be when I dive off the blocks, come to the surface, and then stroke through the water easily, holding my elbows high, both on recovery and under the water. In my imagination, my stroke is strong, fluid, and moves me along easily. When I get to the actual race, it usually goes along this way for the first half or until I begin to tire. Then I have to force things and push harder, at the same time swimming slower, but the imaging always helps me through the first part of these races where I seem to have a special feeling and affinity for the water. It also helps to a degree in the latter part of the race as well, if only because the image of what I'm supposed to be doing remains as a goal I may be temporarily unable to attain, but it keeps my stroke together. Sometimes, however, there are those wonderful days when the imagery carries through for the whole race. Then you have a special feeling beyond just the heightened sensations of the water—the feelings that come with knowing you've done your best!

Work with Your Best Stroke

When trying to develop a feel for the water, it's important to work with your best stroke. That way, you will be more relaxed. For most of us, freestyle (crawl) will be the stroke of choice. But whatever your choice, working on gaining distance per stroke will help you develop this elusive and all-important feel. In freestyle and backstroke, emphasize rolling as you seek to make efficient long strokes. You will be swimming fairly slowly now, but think long, and try to learn and feel from the water. In breaststroke, get a good glide from your kick and make strong, definitive motions with your arms and try to feel the water as it slides by. It may sound harder than it really is, but be relaxed. As in all aspects of swimming, staying relaxed is basic; by relaxing, you open up your senses to the feel of the water.

I would caution lap swimmers that butterfly is probably not a good stroke to use if you're trying to develop kinesthetic feedback from the water. The stroke is enough of a struggle for most of us just to get through a length or two of the pool. The workout swimmer who can swim this stroke in a relaxed way is a rarity.

Hand Paddles and Other Ideas

Hand paddles can also help us gain a greater feel for the water. They tend to put a work overload on the hands and arms, which seems to translate into biofeedback messages. These messages somehow seem to reach the unthinking part of the brain as sensations of the water, its resistance and the pathways through which the hands must travel.

When using hand paddles, don't rush your strokes; keep them long and try to feel the water. If you break your workout into a series of short swims (sets) and allow a few seconds rest between each, you will be fresher throughout your workout. Think about feeling the water, but when you're thinking about this, just try to savor the feeling. Don't dwell on it too hard with your conscious brain. Let the feelings come. Stay relaxed.

Fist swimming can also help. A swimmer can learn to accelerate his hands through the water, to keep his elbows high, and to stroke long with fist drills. I find that this drill makes me feel very slow and uncoordinated while doing it, but upon opening my hands again, there is a sensation of heightened feel for the water.

Underwater push offs and kicking can help. Push off from the wall, and try to glide underwater for distance, adding your kick as you begin to slow down. This drill should be repeated several times. Think about your body and its relationship to the water. Try to feel the point where you're beginning to go slower after your push off. Using swim fins, both for these kicking drills and for some of your actual swimming can also heighten your kinesthetic awareness in the water.

Strength training can sometimes help us gain greater feel in the water. It can also be counterproductive, however, if we're not careful how we do our dry-land weight exercises. Care must be taken not to overdo it; too much pure strength work can cause muscle tightness and soreness that will run counter to gaining feel for the water. It can also result in muscle bulk that is detrimental to feel and good swimming. In strength training, it's important to emphasize the muscle groups that come into play in swimming. I have two points of advice for any swimmer about to embark on dry-land strength work: find a competent trainer who can guide you and try to do weights or use machines in ways that mimic the muscle action of swimming.

Even if you're one of those folks who do not possess great feel for the water, all is not lost. You can still be a good lap swimmer, gaining both pleasure and benefit from your swimming. I think of my late cousin, Pete. He and I had been good friends for most of our lives, and he was instrumental in my early involvement in competitive swimming—but that's another story told elsewhere in this book.

I first became aware that Pete was a workout swimmer when we were both in our late fifties. He showed up one morning at the Brown University pool in one of the "early bird" lanes. Pete always possessed remarkable strength and though heavily muscled was not particularly gifted athletically. Further, when he began his swimming workouts, his natural feel for the water was practically nil. This was undoubtedly related to his muscular build and innate awkwardness. Yet he returned to the pool day after day, stubbornly working, increasing his yardage, seeking help, developing his breathing, rhythm, and lengthening his arm pull. He used both hand paddles and swim fins in his training. Mostly by dint of his own efforts and with only an occasional tip from me, he progressed quite rapidly to the solid exercise benefit level and, until his death, took a good measure of pride in his status as an established lap swimmer. He never competed on the Masters circuit, but he noted and commented to me on both his increased muscular flexibility and improved cardiovascular fitness. And he thoroughly enjoyed his forty minutes a day in the pool.

I know that my cousin's feel for the water increased along with his improvement as a swimmer. In fact, it seems clear to me that improved feel for the water was a key reason he was able to become a better swimmer. His story is solid proof that improvements in feel for the water and better swimming are possible through hard work even if your build-and-body type are not naturally suited for the sport.

Chapter 8

Clara: Pure Drive

Just a small portion of the determination it takes to become an Olympian can make us all better swimmers.

Clara is an old friend. She's also one of the most seriously competitive people I've ever met. She first came into my life when I was a freshman at Brown. Joe Watmough, our coach, had come to the university from the Olneyville Boys Club where he had compiled a marvelous record, developing an inordinate number of world-class swimmers, including three Olympians. These achievements were truly remarkable, considering the bare-bones facility that was his home base. Clara Lamore was the most recent of those elite swimmers.

Joe had been hired as Brown's coach a year or so before I entered the university, but despite moving up College Hill to Brown, he maintained his coaching relationship with Clara. She did not train regularly with us because in that day and age we men swam in the buff. Joe, being a shrewd taskmaster, however, often arranged special Sunday morning workouts for us during the season. We were instructed to wear swimsuits, and Clara was usually on hand to train with us for these special sessions. Her presence always meant harder workouts as our fragile male egos would invariably attempt to rise to the challenge of this fantastic female swimmer who could outswim most of us.

It was 1947, and she was looking forward to the 1948 Olympics and was working very hard. Clara excelled in all the strokes with special strength in backstroke, breaststroke, and the individual medley. At that time in the development of swimming, breaststrokers were beginning to use the frog kick and butterfly arm stroke with its full, under-the-body arm pull, and long over-the-water recovery. Clara was America's top female swimmer in breaststroke, still swimming this specialty in the older classic breaststroke style. Even then she was a very focused and determined individual.

She was also a very attractive young lady, and I'm sure many of us developed crushes, despite the fact that she was beating most of us in our workouts, as we toiled through these long Sunday training sessions. Joe was an insistent chaperone; and no real relationships, social or otherwise, developed. In any case, Clara seemed far too intensely driven toward her Olympic quest for anything else. She trained with us in a spirit of competition and good humor. She went on to make the Olympic team, and while she did not medal, she was the top U.S. finisher in her breaststroke event, scoring a laudable seventh place.

At a gathering, some fifty years after her Olympic success, Clara and I found a quiet corner suitable for old reminiscences. Our discussion sharpened my perspective somewhat. "Your roommate, what a hunk! But he wouldn't give me the time of day!" she said, confessing to a little crush of her own. "But Joe kept everyone in line," she added.

Clara also recounted some of her Olympic experiences, which I discovered were marked with a measure of frustration. "There were only five events for women and six for men—no individual medley, my best event. At the time, Joe told me he didn't know what I should swim. He finally decided on the two-hundred-meter breaststroke. In the trials, I was the top American and made the team without any problem, but of course, I was still swimming classic breaststroke. I had problems in England with the three Dutch girls who were all swimming butterfly breaststroke, which was just coming in and which is a good deal faster than conventional breaststroke. To this day, I still think those Dutch girls were cheating on their kicks." She recounted with a smile, "They were getting that modern dolphin lift, but no judge would disqualify them in the Olympics."

Then Clara confessed to an element of frustration on another score, "Bob Kiphuth (the American Olympic men's coach) evidently paid for airline tickets for the men's team, but the women went to Europe by boat with no training for a week!" But she was not bitter, "That's just the way things were in 1948."

After the Olympics, I did not see Clara for a time. She entered the convent, then after six years found her vocation to be uncertain and was released from her vows. Next, there was a marriage, which ended tragically seven years later with the death of her naval-officer husband in Italy. Her life continued, and she became a teacher and well-regarded guidance counselor in the public schools in Cranston, Rhode Island. She swam occasionally, but it was not until she reached her midfifties that Clara decided it was time to become a competitor again.

No longer Clara Lamore, but now Clara Walker, she entered into the Masters swim scene with a vengeance. She didn't just break national and world records in her age-group, she put them in a whole new universe. She was clearly the super swimmer of her age-group. She swam all the events, long and short, all four strokes, and individual medleys where in view of her strength in each of the strokes, she particularly shined. Clara found a new coach, John O'Neill, head coach for men and women at Providence College, and she trained with the same dedication we saw back in the late '40s when her goal was the Olympics. Now her objective was to set those national and world records, which she proceeded to do in four age-groups during some twenty years of Masters swimming competition.

I'm sure Clara must have been a fine teacher. I know from remarks I've heard from mutual friends that she had an excellent rapport with her students and engendered much loyalty and respect among them. When I meet people for the first time, they invariably ask me if I know Clara. While her fame in Rhode Island's relatively small community may be a factor in the way people regard Clara, more likely the fact that she holds a genuine interest in people, especially her students, younger folks generally and those she counts as friends, gets more to the heart of why people respond so favorably to her. She has always shown an interest in my swimming although I often feel a flash of chagrin when I'm not able to answer positively to her inevitable query: "Did you break any records at the meet?"

Her interest in swimming is just one facet of her personality. Clara tends to hide her intellect, and it is only after you get to know her quite well that you come to realize that she is a complicated and very thoughtful lady of considerable brain power. Possessing a positive personality and a fine sense of humor, she is also fiercely independent as might be expected of one who has lived alone for a number of decades.

At national and world championships, it was always a pleasure to be on the same mixed relay with Clara. Mixed relays involve two men and two women. At these championships, two mixed relays are swum—a freestyle relay and a medley relay. In the medley relay, all four strokes are used, so a certain amount of strategy takes place involving assigning swimmers to strokes. In Clara's case, it didn't make much difference because she was so good in them all. Sometimes, we felt it was almost unfair. With Clara on our mixed relay team, we had a person whose speed rivaled most men! And she always joined in with a sense of genuine enthusiasm.

She would take special joy in leading off on backstroke and staying right with men in adjoining lanes. "I didn't let him get much of a lead, did I?" She would enthuse with a somewhat self-congratulatory, rhetorical question, delivered in response to celebratory cheers from her teammates. Actually, leading off, more often than not, she would win those short backstroke face-offs with the men in adjoining lanes in those mixed relays.

As good as Clara is, she is not a natural swimmer. She is a "made" swimmer. Of course, she is a product of her own dedication and willingness to work. That's always the way, but in Clara's case, she is an athlete who was able to develop an average natural talent far beyond what would ordinarily be expected. As I came to know her better, I began to understand her tremendous ability to focus and her willingness to drive her body through various pain thresholds in order to reach her goals.

And that's the real point of Clara's story—an example of what dedication and hard work can achieve. Clara's talent is the ability to set goals and then, utilizing her own special, even unique ability to focus, move toward those aims with singular purpose. In Clara's case, there were many sacrifices in other aspects of her personal and professional life in order to meet her objectives in swimming.

Now having just cleared the eighty mark, Clara can easily be mistaken for women fifteen to twenty years younger. Short of stature, she is trim, in obvious good health and very fit. Her step is firm and quick, and she carries herself with a certain athletic grace. Her youthful-appearing fitness would seem to be another outcome of her dedication to the exercise of her sport.

The suggestion here is not that we should all pattern ourselves after Clara, seeking the same kind of stardom. Far from it. The lesson, however, is to underscore that average talent can produce excellence if the dedication is there. It's a question of goal setting and willingness to follow through and even sacrifice. Most of us would not set our objectives so high nor, in all likelihood, possess the ability to focus so strongly. We all must set our own goals and follow our own pathways in these matters. Clara's story tells us that athletic improvement is possible through hard work, despite whatever physical shortcomings we may possess. The lesson goes far beyond mere athletics of course.

In Clara's case, a very special award came to her in 1997. She was one of two Masters swimmers inducted into the International Swimming Hall of Fame in Fort Lauderdale, Florida. They were the first two swimmers inducted out of recognition for their Masters achievements. Clara's case for induction was well documented as she was the present or past holder of 184 world records and 468 national records over four age-groups in Masters swimming. In the world of swimming, induction into this Hall of Fame is perhaps the ultimate honor and obviously highly deserved in her case!

As a postscript to Clara's story, she is presently a lap swimmer, having succumbed to a bout of shoulder problems. As she puts it with typical good humor, "I'm just swimming for fun, relaxation, and basic conditioning right now, but if my shoulders will let me, I'll be back with you competitors one day."

Clara is a marvelous example of a goal-driven individual. Very few of us can expect to have the drive for excellence that she has exhibited in her life. She has achieved much both in and beyond swimming. The point of Clara's story here is to show how hard work can have its result. For most lap swimmers and would-be lap swimmers, a small portion of Clara's drive could pay huge dividends in improvement in the water.

Section 2

Different Strokes and Other Information

Chapter 9

Backstroke

Backstroke isn't for everyone, but I see lots of lap swimmers flipping over on their backs for a few strokes at least. Most of them could use some help. The view from the backstroker's perspective is a lot wider and generally more interesting than that found in facedown swimming, particularly outdoors.

Backstroke is an upside down and backward stroke. You watch where you've been rather than where you're going! Even so, correctly swum, it is perhaps the most graceful of all the strokes. We older folks tend to conjure up visions of the beautiful Esther Williams moving effortlessly through the water, backstroking her way to movie stardom. Ah, if only we could all emulate the grace of an Esther Williams!

One of my early swimming memories is my introduction to the dramatic Yale University exhibition pool and seeing for the first time a world-class backstroker in action. That pool was built auditorium style, with steeply banked seats. Entering as a spectator at the top level, as I did that day, is very impressive. You walk through a portal and look down—way down. There at the bottom, somewhere seemingly miles away, is this beautiful spectacle of bluish water surrounded by a white deck. What caught my eye that day way down there was a tall male form doing backstroke in what appeared to be slow motion.

The tall male form was Alan Stack, then America's top backstroker. Stack, perhaps six feet seven, had a nice, clean, athletic build and long arms, which he moved with singular grace and deliberation in the water. He was obviously getting the most out of each stroke as he worked out. I was far too much of a swimming neophyte myself to know anything about stroke counts, but I remember my amazement at how few Stack seemed to take as he moved through the water. His signature was grace with power, something for us all to strive for no matter what strokes we swim.

Breathing for Backstroke

Very few of us will ever swim the backstroke like Alan Stack, and I'm sure many of us are struggling with various aspects of our aquatic skills. For the swimmer who has not yet developed full confidence in breath control, the backstroke has one huge advantage. Since your face is out of the water the entire time, you don't have to worry much about breathing. It will happen fairly naturally although those new to the stroke may tend to breathe more often than ideal. Coaches generally advise their swimmers to inhale only once during the arm cycle, usually at the end of the recovery for one arm, just prior to the hand entry, and to let the air out somewhat gradually during the rest of the arm cycle. Not developing a regular breathing pattern can result in ragged, uncoordinated breathing and inefficient oxygen intake as well as a failure to exhale properly. This will result in shortness of breath and difficult swimming.

Backstroke, or at least back crawl, can be viewed as an upside-down front crawl. The arms operate in sequence—first one and then the other—with timing that is similar to that of freestyle. There is a form of backstroke, which is more of an inverted breaststroke, involving the frog kick, or its "whip frog" derivative, and a double arm-stroking motion. This is a fairly effective way of swimming that has adherents primarily among pure breaststrokers who have limited flutter-kicking ability. This chapter will, however, deal only with the more common back crawl.

Backstroke. Illustration shows left arm beginning stroking action while right arm starts its recovery. Swimmer is rolling to his left.

Generally speaking, backstrokers are pretty good kickers, and that's probably why so many of them at the competitive level are also good sprinters, freestyle sprinting calling for a big flutter kick. The six-beat kick is the standard from which few stray in backstroke. Somehow, the six beat just naturally fits the back crawl. Again, six beats means six kicks for each full-arm cycle—three kicks on each side for the arm on the same side.

So far, it sounds fairly simple. You just prone out on your back in the water, start your kick, and begin stroking. Your head position should be reasonably deep in the water. Holding your head too high will cause your buttocks and legs to drop, creating extra drag. Most backstrokers hold the waterline just barely under their ears; the body will be in a fairly straight alignment, the hips just an inch or two below the surface, and the chest just above the surface. Variations in body position will occur from person to person, depending upon physique and buoyancy. The most common error in backstroke positioning is holding the head too high. The result is a "sitting" position with increased drag.

The Kick

The kick is similar to that described in the chapter on kicking except reversed (upside down). When kicking, you want to be sure that your knees do not break the surface of the water. If you find you're making this error, it will be necessary to make body adjustments by raising or lowering your head or to change your kick to emphasize more strongly what is now the downbeat where the leg straightens as you apply force toward the bottom of the pool. The action is described in the chapter titled "The Flutter Kick for Freestyle." Again, you should remember to keep your legs relaxed, especially the feet, ankles, and knees as you apply the power.

Backstroke. Illustration shows backstroke kick—essentially front crawl upside down (**feet should remain just below surface of the water during the kick**)

The best way to practice backstroke kicking is to simply lie on your back in the water and start kicking. You should try to stretch your arms ahead of you in the water, clasping your hands so that your arms find a position fairly tight at each side of your head. This will ensure a more correct, streamlined body position in the water and force you to work a little harder in order to make progress. And be aware of your knees. Keep them underwater. If you're just starting with your backstroke, you may find holding one hand at your side easier at first, but try to move to the hands ahead position described here as you get used to this backstroke-kicking exercise.

The Arms: High Elbows Again

While the legs take on a more important role in backstroke than they do in the front crawl, you will need to count on your arms for at least 80 percent of your momentum. Swimmers learning the backstroke sometimes try to pull too deeply. Much of the pull should be to the side, but again as in freestyle, there is arm bending at the elbows, the high elbow position, and a restraightening of the arm in the water just prior to recovery—an S pattern throughout the stroke. And like freestyle, backstroke being the other "long axis stroke," controlled body roll is important. This more easily allows the larger muscles of the back, chest, and hips to come into play.

Backstroke. Illustration shows nice straight arm recovery

At the recovery phase, the swimmer will release the water below the hips and use a straight-arm recovery to a position directly ahead and slightly outside of the shoulder. The hand will be placed in the water with the little finger entering first so that the palm will face outward. Next comes the "catch" phase where the hand should rotate so that the palm is facing more toward the bottom of the pool, and the swimmer will make a strong push down and backward. The hand will drop below the surface, partially because of the downward push but perhaps more because of body roll toward the pulling side. As your stroke continues, your elbow will flex. This is the point where you need to remember to keep your elbow "high." At the midpoint of the stroke there may be as much as a ninety-degree bend at the elbow! Here, your hand will once again be near the surface. Then a straightening should occur as your stroke changes from pull to a push backward to the recovery point. The back of the hand will lead the exit from the water.

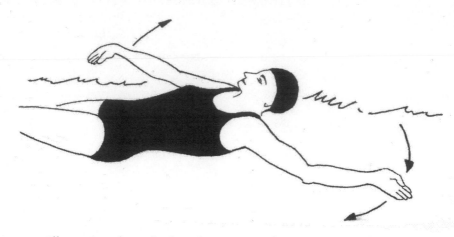

Illustration shows backstroker timing of arms, and approximate head position in water

Just as in freestyle, the bent "high elbow" underwater sets up arm alignment to create maximum leverage for the application of force through the power phase of the stroke occurring as the arm straightens and you move from a pull to a push in the stroke. There is a natural, elongated S pattern to this stroke when viewed from the side. The elongation is emphasized during the last part of the stroke when the wrist turns inward, thumb pointing toward the hip. A pressing downward of the hand should occur as the arm is extended backward to the release point just before exiting the water for recovery. This downward press seems to initiate the proper rolling action for the stroke. The S begins at entry, then the hand drops forming the first loop in the S, next the hand returns toward the surface as the elbow flexes during the midpoint of the stroke, and finally the second loop is described as the hand is pushed back and downward toward the exit point.

The flexed elbow is still thought of as a high elbow since its position in relation to the body is similar to the high elbow described as correct for the front crawl. More accurately, I suppose, the elbow in backstroke could be termed a "low" elbow since in its bent position it will be positioned considerably below the hand, which is now much closer to the surface. (This bit of confused terminology is just part of this upside down and backward stroke.) Remember that the high elbow in backstroke will perform the same function as it does in freestyle, keeping the hand and arm in a strong position and ensuring that the hand will lead the stroke after the entry, catch and up to the midpoint of the pulling action.

Maglischo breaks down the correct backstroke pull in fairly simple a, b, c, d, e, f, and with instructions:

a. *Place your hand in the water directly in front of your shoulder with your palm facing out.*

b. *After it enters, make a strong catch by turning your hand down and out and pushing down on the water.*

c. *Initial downsweep. Once the catch is made, sweep your hand down and out, turning your hand toward the bottom as you do.*
    Roll your shoulders, hips, and legs toward the downsweeping arm.

d. *Upsweep. When your hand passes its deepest point, turn your palm upward and sweep it upward, inward, and backward in a diagonal path until your arm is flexed nearly ninety degrees.*

e. *Final downsweep. As your hand approaches the surface, sweep it backward and downward past your thigh. Pitch your palm downward and outward as you do.*

f. *Recovery. When your arm is extended at the end of the downsweep, lift your shoulder out of the water to initiate the recovery. Your arm will follow your shoulder. Your hand should leave the water on its side with palm facing inward. Recover your arm directly overhead, rotating your palm outward as it passes overhead.*

Rolling

Good backstrokers swim with a very pronounced roll. At the same time, the head is held stationary. To an observer, the swimmer will appear to be stroking with this rolling action taking place in a circular motion back and forth around the head and neck. It's almost as though the backstroker was held together by a wire running from the top of the head to the crotch. Everything revolves—half revolutions—with the imaginary wire holding things together at the center. This rolling is a good deal more pronounced than in freestyle and can be as much as forty-five degrees away from the horizontal plane. A good backstroker, swimming at competitive speeds, will spend very little time in a horizontal position, instead moving through a level plane in a continuous rolling motion.

Backstroke. Illustration shows backstroker rolling to right as that arm pulls in the water, elbow bent (high), left arm recovering (water not shown)

Watching the Flags

Since you will have trouble seeing where you're going in backstroke, it's important to learn the landmarks of your pool. Most pools today have backstroke flags situated five yards (or in the case of meter pools, five meters) from the end of the pool. These are there for your safety. Swimming backstroke at a good clip and banging your head or hand on the end of the pool can be painful. The flags also work as guides for turns for competitive swimmers and are especially crucial for outdoor pools where there is no ceiling but instead, sky and clouds. There will be more information on turns for various strokes in the chapter titled "Turns" later in the book.

Making It Fun

Backstroke can be a fun way of swimming even though some folks may tell you they don't like swimming backward, seeing where they're coming from rather than where they're going. The pleasant thing is your face is out of the water, and while it might not be the ultimate and correct way of swimming for competition, you can look around and enjoy the scenery—something not possible with the other strokes. Most coaches would kill me for saying this, but generally, lap swimmers can look around and "smell the roses" when swimming backstroke. This is a way of swimming where you can see more than just the bottom of a swimming pool. I see it as an "enjoy life" way of swimming. If, however, you are a serious swimmer, take heed of what I've said earlier in the chapter, keep your head on straight—literally—and avoid the temptation of looking around as you do your laps.

Backstroke. Illustration shows swimmer with nice rolling action to left as arm strokes with good elbow bend. Head is a little high. (Looking around too much?)

Chapter 10

Breaststroke

Breaststroke is a wonderful stroke for the marginal swimmer. You can swim a long time with it, and the breathing aspects are simple. But for the breaststroke competitor, it's a far more taxing world.

There's no question about it: good breaststrokers are a different breed. Swimmers who excel in the other strokes often have trouble with the breaststroke, and likewise, really good breaststrokers are often not particularly competent in the other strokes. It's probably that there are certain physiological differences in the make-up of the true breaststroker compared to what we might see in regular swimmers.

From the above, you can infer correctly that the breaststroke is a stroke at which I'm not proficient. Still, I have great admiration for those competitive marvels who do well with it. There is beauty in watching an elite breaststroker in action. The kick is strong, and the pulling action causes a reverse rooster tail of water to flow forward off the swimmer's chest as the competitor surges ahead with each thrust of arms and legs.

Phil Whitten had some interesting words about the breaststroke in his book, *The Complete Book of Swimming*:

> *Breaststroke is the enigmatic stroke. Regarded by novices as the easiest stroke, it is acknowledged by experts to be the most difficult. The breaststroke is used for relaxation by casual swimmers, but when swum competitively, it burns more calories than any other stroke, with the possible exception of the butterfly.*

An interesting commentary and very accurate. The breaststroke is probably the way people first began swimming, and the first person to swim the English Channel, Matthew Webb, in 1875 used it. The stroke has undergone much development, particularly in recent years; and today, there are several styles that are in vogue, each with its adherents. We'll try to keep it reasonably simple here.

The Kick

In breaststroke, the kick is critically important—far more so than in any other stroke. When swimmers like me complain that they are not good breaststrokers, it's almost always because, for one reason or another, we have poor kicks. In my case, I can blame it on a trick knee that protests when I demand too much breaststroke kicking from it. Having a disability to fall back on can be a great convenience. It gives me the luxury of being able to take the realistically untenable position that except for my bad knee, I would have been one of the truly great breaststrokers in Masters swimming.

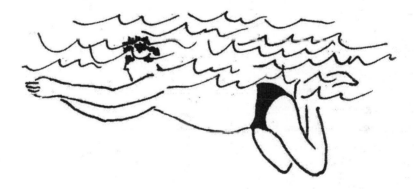

Breastroke. Illustration shows breastroker with arms extended, heels at buttocks as thrust phase of the kick begins.

One of the more recent developments in the breaststroke involves the kick. Originally, we were taught to bring our knees up toward our chests and to kick out in a V motion, separating the knees, legs, and feet and then bringing the legs together in a squeezing motion. That has changed to what is called the whip kick. This modern, more effective kick is used by virtually all competitors today. The major differences in the whip and the frog kick being an emphasis on bringing the feet farther up toward the buttocks rather than simply dropping the knees. The result is a kick with far less separation in the knees and, at the same time, more emphasis on turning the feet outward, with the feet providing propulsion in a propeller-like motion.

You should start the whip kick by bringing your feet back toward your buttocks, at the same time dropping your knees and hips. Once your lower legs are close to your buttocks, you should turn your feet out, then down, bringing the feet and legs together. Then there is a pause or glide in the kicking action while the arms stroke. Your hips will rise slightly, and a lifting action of your legs will occur.

It sounds simple, but the main key is that you must feel the water when you whip against it as you bring your legs together. It is amazing how strongly the good practitioners of this kick are able to move! Maglischo argues convincingly in his book, *Swimming Faster*, that much of the propulsive force generated from the whip kick occurs from the use of a propeller-like action from the feet:

> *Breaststrokers use their feet as propellers, rotating them outward, downward, and inward in a circular path. Although some backward motion occurs, the feet do not push directly backward against the water.*

This "propeller theory," now being debated by coaches, would seem to get us to the cutting edge of modern coaching concept. I will leave it that the action of turning the feet outward when they are lifted close to the buttocks is the correct move and should be followed immediately by a circular motion as the feet and legs are brought together.

Despite what the good breaststrokers say, it's not always easy. My advice is to get out the kickboard and do lots of breaststroke kicking. Make this part—the kick—of your breaststroke automatic since the kick is so important that you need to learn to do it naturally without having to think about it.

The Arms

Of course, your arms are important too. And here too, there has been a good deal of stroke development in recent years, particularly as rule changes in the competitive world have meant certain coaching reactions aimed at squeezing a few precious tenths of seconds in lowered times. A rule change that now allows the swimmers to lower their heads underneath the surface of the water as they reach forward has allowed swimmers to employ a greater amount of undulation or dolphin action in their swimming. Here too, a fine line of distinction must be drawn. Too much undulation is a ground for disqualification in racing. But for the lap swimmer, disqualification is not a problem. Learning correct leg, arm, and breathing actions in all the strokes should be enough of a burden to carry without the worry of disqualification, something that only occurs in the world of racing.

Actually, the arm action in the breaststroke is fairly simple, perhaps the reason—in Whitten's words—beginners find it the easiest stroke. You should pull, starting with your arms extended in front and approximately six inches below the surface, using simultaneous action in both arms. Your arms should describe a more or less upside-down "heart-shaped" motion as you pull out and downward. The first motion will be the "outsweep," which goes to a point just beyond shoulder width. Here, the catch phase occurs, and your motion should continue downward and then backward. From the point of catch and through the downsweep, you will feel a definite lift of your shoulders and body. Next, the insweep motion should occur where you bring your hands together and up and then move directly to recovery and extension. There is no pause. Your hands should be under your chin and your elbows fairly close together underneath your chest. You release the water and slide your hands forward, trying to maintain a streamlined position in the water as you reach for full extension and begin the next stroke. The illustrations on these pages should help.

Breastroke. Illustration shows swimmer finishing the insweep of arms to a point under the chin. Note the arms pull back only to the shoulders.

High Elbows Again

As in the other strokes we have discussed, the high elbows are critical. Neophyte breaststrokers also are surprised that the arm stroke occurs almost entirely in front of the shoulders with the hands going no farther back than the shoulders. Pulling back too far is one of the classic errors seen in practitioners of this stroke. This stroke flaw disrupts the rhythmic flow of the stroke and creates negative drag forces as the arms are recovered.

The propulsive force of the arm stroke increases through the outsweep, downsweep, and insweep phases of the stroke. The outsweep should be quite wide—about twice shoulder width. This will set up a strong downsweep and insweep. During the outsweep, your palms should face generally out, angled at approximately sixty degrees. At the end of the outsweep, the catch is made, and your hands should change pitch to a more downward and backward angle. This pitch will hold throughout the downsweep to take advantage of "lift," an important propulsive force for swimmers. During the insweep, the angle of the hands changes so that the palms will now more nearly face each other as the hands move together into the recovery phase.

The changing pitch of the hands is somewhat complicated. The ability to make the subtle shifts of hand angle correctly is one of the aspects that separates the elite swimmers from the ordinary. These pitch changes are sometimes referred to as sculling motions and are initiated more by feel of the water than by any forced mechanical action. In the paragraph above, there is a reference to lift. This is the same kind of lift force that allows an airplane to fly. Swimmers don't necessarily feel this force, but it can be demonstrated by making simple sculling motions in the water with your hands while lying prone in the water. Sculling will move you forward—or even backward—depending upon the pitch of your hands.

Much of the above is probably a little esoteric for most of us since it takes us once again to the fringes of coaching theory where coaches seek to understand all forces that come into play to make their swimmers move just a little faster in the water. Experimentation in any stroke will help us find a more correct pitch to our hands. This is especially important in the breaststroke because the shortened aspect of the stroke demands a greater degree of efficiency for successful swimming. Developing a good feel for the water—something I have mentioned before—is especially important in helping us make these corrections. Some of us clearly have better feel for the water than others, but it is a skill that can be developed. An earlier chapter is devoted to this, but here it is suffice to point out that this aspect of feel will help you develop good timing in your stroke, and good timing results in more efficiency, grace, and ultimately speed.

Putting It Together

The timing of arms and kick is fairly simple. Most lap swimmers are going to be swimming the breaststroke at a more leisurely pace, and I recommend the use of an extended glide after the recovery and extension in the kick, bringing the arms into the equation as you begin to lose momentum. The rhythm then becomes kick, glide, pull, kick, glide, pull. It should fit in together quite naturally. Modern competitive swimmers today do not use the extended glide form of breaststroke although we can be fairly certain that Matt Webb used plenty of it for his 1875 English Channel crossing.

Today's competitors use rapid-fire variations of the stroke described above, including the dolphin action of body undulation, which takes the stroke close to the limits of its rules. The wave variation of the breaststroke calls for an arm recovery above the water, arms still directly in front of the head, to eliminate drag during arm recovery. In short, the competitive level breaststroke is a very taxing stroke, just as Whitten told us at the beginning of this chapter.

Breathing

Less complicated than all the stroke concepts discussed above is breathing. Whether you employ the more comfortable glide form of breaststroke or one of the rapid-fire variations of the competitive style, breathing is critically important. Inhaling should begin immediately when your mouth clears the water and end when your head and shoulders are at their highest point, during the insweep. Exhaling takes place during the rest of the stroke sequence, primarily as you extend your arms with your face in the water looking toward the pool's bottom. You should breathe every stroke. This will ensure that you have a good supply of oxygen, and it will also enhance the rhythm of your breaststroke.

The paradox in breaststroke is that it can be a nice, relaxed change in our swimming, or it can be a fast-paced, rather violent, energy-consuming competitive stroke. Most of us will prefer to swim the former and watch the latter! But for those who have tons of pent-up energy to burn, there's always the less-relaxed style as typified by the breaststroke used in competition.

Chapter 11

Butterfly

This stroke is really only for those lap swimmers and triathletes looking for a special challenge.

A couple of years ago, I walked into the locker room after a hard butterfly workout, complaining about my back. A lot of dolphin kicking can put a serious strain on the lower back where a good deal of the initial motion for the kick originates. Someone I didn't know too well heard me complaining and said something to the effect, "You damn fool, if it hurts you that much, why do you swim it?"

The only response I could muster was a somewhat foolish sounding, "Well, I've got to. That's what I'm good at."

Realistically, you can only push the body so far. That's why I recommend lap swimmers stay away from the butterfly, at least until they become truly competent freestyle swimmers. In rebuttal, however, there's a swimmer I see occasionally at one of the pools I frequent whose workout is almost entirely butterfly. He has a relaxed but deliberate, long-pulling stroke where he buries his head about a foot below the surface on his arm recovery, utilizing a slow one-beat dolphin kick. He doesn't try for speed, but he can go forever. In the annual "Swim the Bay," across Narragansett Bay, sponsored by Save the Bay Inc., my friend does butterfly throughout the mile and three-quarter swim. He's an exception, and I will admit to a spark of envy. I can't swim it that way, and I've won lots of one hundred yards and one-hundred-meter events nationally and at world championship meets. I have to train long and painfully to go even that far, and I've quit even trying to compete at two hundred yards because I felt too close to death the few times I've tried that distance. My problem, I suppose, is that I haven't figured out how to swim the butterfly slowly. I've tried my friend's way, but it just doesn't work for me.

A Basic Description

People have asked me why the stroke is called butterfly. I don't really have the answer. Perhaps it's because someone watching saw the two arms recovering over the water together and was reminded of a butterfly's wings in flight. Who knows?

Butterfly is a lot like double-arm freestyle. The arms and legs work together. Each arm describes motions similar to those of the front crawl, including the S pattern underneath and high elbows. Since both arms work simultaneously, there can be no body roll, and the stroke is therefore shallower. The arms must also recover together, requiring a good deal of shoulder flexibility so that the arms and hands will clear the surface on recovery. Some people use a straight-arm recovery; others recover over the water with high elbows. I use the latter method, which for me seems to set up the high elbow position needed in the early stages of the pull.

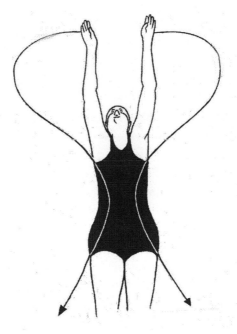

Butterfly. Illustration shows "S" pattern of arms under body in butterfly stroke

The entry point for the arms is just outside of shoulder width. Your thumbs should enter the water first, just as in freestyle. After entry, your hands will move forward and somewhat together to the catch. This is quickly followed by the outsweep. Next comes the downsweep and insweep under the body where the hands will be quite close together again. This is followed by the upsweep phase, which follows through to the release point below the bottom of your suit as your arms straighten and recovery occurs. Your shoulders should be mostly out of the water during the recovery phase as a good deal of lift takes place at this point in the stroke.

Butterfly. Illustration shows swimmer beginning the arm recovery

Butterfly Kicking

The kick is much like a flutter kick except that both legs work together, with much of the initiation of force coming from the lower back. The standard for the stroke is two kicks for each arm cycle, the first of the two kicks being somewhat stronger than the second. The swimmer's low head position during the first kick allows the hips to move up and forward, giving the illusion of a stronger first kick. Maglischo cautions that the swimmer should put about the same effort into both kicks.

The key in butterfly is the changing body position, timing the arm pull with the two kicks and the all-important breathing at the proper point. I will go into more detail, but I know when I'm swimming this stroke, I don't think about any of this. It all just seems to happen naturally. My general advice would be to concentrate on your arms and fit the two kicks in where it seems comfortable. Again, as stated in other chapters, I'm a strong believer in isolating the various skills we're learning, and in the case of the dolphin kick, just as in the freestyle kick, I recommend doing lots of kicking with the kickboard and even some underwater kicking with fins.

Butterfly. Illustration shows butterfly swimmer with arms extended, buttocks raised and legs just beginning upward path.

Don't be discouraged if you find the butterfly kick pretty slow going at first. It's not a natural motion, but you'll be surprised at how much speed you'll be able to generate with the dolphin if you keep at it. Once you find you're able to maintain a reasonable pace with the kickboard, you should try some drills, kicking on your side without the board but with your lower arm stretched out in front. Be sure to change sides frequently. This drill will give you a good feel for the motions needed for the dolphin kick. You might also try some underwater kicking without a board. If you happen to be one of those rare people with a natural ability for this kick, you'll find it one of your fastest ways of swimming.

Top competitors in both the butterfly and backstroke are now using lots of underwater dolphin kicking after the start and from the walls on turns. The natural kickers are finding this is faster than swimming their normal strokes on the surface. Backstrokers, of course, do their dolphin kicking in the inverted position in order to stay within the rules. The rules also limit, primarily for safety reasons, the distance a swimmer can stay underwater to fifteen yards or meters after the start or from the walls on turns. The problem is that while underwater kicking is faster for some, the swimmer pays a price in "oxygen debt" for going without air so long. Pushing for too much speed under the water in the early and middle parts of a race often results in tightening up and an extreme slow down at the end of races as the swimmer's stroke comes apart.

In General

But these are problems most lap swimmers will not need to worry about. Still, if you're determined to try the butterfly, it's important to learn the kick and to make sure it's something you're able to do without putting a lot of thought into it. Using your arms properly and coordinating your breathing will take all the concentration most neophyte butterflyers can muster!

Butterfly. Illustration shows swimmer with arm action underway, elbows bent (high) legs beginning downward path

Breathing

That brings us to the important aspect of breathing. Butterfly uses lots of air, so breathing is very important. The act of breathing can affect the rhythm of the stroke. You should inhale at the highest point in your stroke. In correctly swum butterfly, there should be a lifting effect taking place at the end of the pull as you move into the recovery. At that point, you should lift your head in a forward thrusting motion and inhale quickly, then bring your head back down to lead your arms into the entry phase.

Most successful butterflyers breathe directly to the front. One of the risks of breathing to the front, however, is catching a wave in your mouth just as you're trying to inhale. It doesn't happen often, but it's something that goes with the territory, making it especially critical to exhale completely—underwater—before you pick your head up for that quick bite of air. Shortening the time you need for inhaling will cut down the risk of "breathing" water. If you're breathing every other stroke, you need to control the action of exhaling. I usually hold my newly inhaled air as I pull through on the first stroke, then begin to exhale slowly, finally pushing out the rest of the air just as I finish my second arm pull so that I'm fully ready to inhale as I lift my head again.

The raising and lowering of your head in butterfly is an important action for creating the flow necessary to the stroke. Even on nonbreathing strokes, there should be some lifting and lowering of the head. The lowering of the head helps lead the arms back into the water. There is a lunging action here that is critical to the flow of the stroke. When you lower your head, you need to press your chin down to the point where your chest and neck come together. The lifting of your head will help lower your hips, just as the lowering of your head once again will raise them; this action helps to force-feed the butterfly dolphin motion.

In my case, experimentation has proven to me that I get the best results breathing every third arm stroke in the fifty yards or meters and every other stroke when I swim the one hundred. Normally, most Masters competitors swimming two hundred yards or meter races will rely on every-stroke breathing throughout. When I try to breathe every stroke, the timing in my butterfly breaks down, making it very difficult for me to keep swimming. I suppose I could put the screw down a few notches in my training to learn to carry the stroke for the full two hundred, breathing at my normal, every-other-stroke pace, but the training would be too painful and tortuous. Swimming is supposed to be fun!

More on the Arms

While the action of the arms underwater is somewhat similar to that of the front crawl, the stroking and recovery are different. Butterfly—like breaststroke, being a short axis stroke with no body roll—has similar underwater stroking patterns. The butterfly arm stroke compares most closely to the arm action of the breaststroker making the one full, underwater stroke allowed on dive and turn take off. Both strokes share a pronounced outreach, followed by the catch. Other than for the full underwater pull taken after the dive and turns, the breaststroke features a quicker, shorter insweep while the butterfly's insweep is more extended to a release point below the bottom of the bathing suit after which the recovery occurs.

Butterfly. Illustration shows arms under body, elbows bent with
hands close together, legs descending.

Butterflyers should do a good deal of pull work in their workouts to gain
arm strength and conditioning. This means swimming with a pull buoy and
paddles. While it is possible to actually mimic the butterfly stroke with its
simultaneous arm pull, I'm not sure it's necessary or even advisable. Freestyle
pulling is so close to the action needed in butterfly that simply doing enough
front crawl, pull-buoy work is probably all that is necessary.

One of my age-group competitors has done a lot of his fly pulling the other
way, however, completing pull sets in actual butterfly, arms-simultaneous
pulling using paddles. He believes, however, that this was one of the causes
of some shoulder problems he developed. He ended up with surgery. This
stroke puts great demands on the shoulders, particularly where the recovery
action requires good shoulder flexibility, evidently calling for motions that
push right up to the limits of what the human body was built to do. My
advice is to do plenty of regular freestyle pulling, which—because of the
rolling action involved—treats the shoulders more gently.

Timing and a Couple of Tips

You need to be able to feel your way through the stroke. It can't be
blueprinted in any meaningful way that gives the swimmer a road map for

swimming success. Imaging may well be the best route to follow for this stroke. Try to find good butterflyers and study the flow of motion so that the action is ingrained on your nervous system; then perhaps the descriptions here will make more sense. It would be a case of the intellectual aspect—the information of what the stroke is all about—reinforcing the imagery you have absorbed into your own sensory system, the mind and the physical coming together as one.

As far as timing of kicks and arms goes, I have already indicated that it's probably best to concentrate on arms and breathing and to fit the legs in where it seems comfortable. It will probably feel the most comfortable if you begin the downbeat of the first kick as your arms enter the water in front of your head. The downbeat will finish approximately as the catch is made with your hands, with the upbeat of the kick taking place during the downsweep and insweep of the arms. The downbeat of the second kick then is initiated during the upsweep of the arms, the upbeat of this kick taking place along with the recovery.

One of the better ways of working into this stroke is to combine it with freestyle swimming. What you do is push off the wall and take a couple of butterfly strokes and then drop back to freestyle. Decide at the beginning of the workout set how far you plan to swim—for instance, you might decide to swim sixteen lengths, each length of two butterfly strokes and x number of strokes freestyle. You complete the swim, and hopefully the next day, you would be able to do the same swim using three butterfly strokes. The idea is to keep adding the amount of fly you do each day.

While it's not an easy stroke to swim well, the feeling you get from swimming the stroke smoothly and efficiently is one of glorious exaltation. You feel as though you're moving through the water almost effortlessly. Unfortunately, that feeling only lasts for me for the first forty yards or so of a one-hundred-yard race. Then the struggle begins, and it's not a whole lot of fun. Ten yards from the end, your arms don't want to complete the stroke, much less recover through the air and get ready for another painful push through the water. Sometimes to complete the race, I have to put my head down and stop breathing. Otherwise, I'm unable to get my arms through at all, much less make the recovery. As a "golden-aged" swimmer, I'm beginning to question if doing it this way makes good health sense.

Chapter 12

How I Became a Flyer

Pushing the envelope can have its own reward.

Sometimes we find hidden talents we didn't know we had. My comeback into Masters swimming was planned strictly as a freestyler. My thought was to do it as a sprinter so I wouldn't have to train much. That was my lazy streak showing, but it didn't work out for the simple reason I just wasn't fast enough. The gift of speed is something you either have or don't have, and mine is only modest. That meant middle distance and longer would be my freestyle forte all mixed in with a good seasoning of hard training. You just don't try to swim those long races without putting in a lot of pool time.

Once I had made the mental switch, started to train, and had thrown away my cigarettes, I was quite happy with the reality of my talents. I'd been a middle distance swimmer in college, so it was only logical that I'd still be one. After turning fifty, I found I was pretty competitive with the better distance swimmers in my age-group—not head and shoulders above standout, but not bad either! I was reasonably happy about my first national Masters meet with five silvers and a gold in the one hundred free, but then I found out about relays.

I made the club two-hundred-yard freestyle relay but was left off the medley. I would have to find another stroke if I was going to make that one because I was far down on the club depth chart for fifty-yard freestylers. Relays include ten-year spreads, so I was swimming on the forty-five-plus team. Thinking about this challenge, I first looked at backstroke as a possibility. I'd once been the State of RI AAU champion in the 150-yard backstroke when the two big studs in Rhode Island both failed to appear for a race which was to have been a head-to-head showdown for a couple of the best backstrokers the state had ever produced. But that was twenty-six years earlier!

A couple of fifty-yard backstroke events in local mini meets left me with a sinking feeling: my backstroke was not going to do it. I hadn't totally given up on the idea; I can be a pretty stubborn cuss even when facing reality. But then a notice for an upcoming mini meet at a local YMCA pool listed the one-hundred-individual medley as one of the events. There weren't any of the events I normally swim listed, so I began to think about that one hundred IM.

Since I'd never even tried modern butterfly, the big question in my mind was whether I could make that first twenty-five yards of the pool swimming butterfly. The other three strokes would not be a problem; I'd been working on my backstroke and I did know how to do a slow, inefficient breaststroke, which included a pretty good turn and push off. If I could get through the fly, I knew I'd be okay. Since I had a couple of weeks, I tried the new (to me) stroke with its strange dolphin kick that initially I found completely confounding. My first attempts at butterfly felt awkward and confused, but it did carry me forward in the water. The use of the kickboard working on the dolphin motion was somewhat frustrating, but just the same, productive. It was frustrating because my kick was so awful, but productive because some improvement with practice was apparent even after a few days.

At the meet, I dove in and stroked with reasonable smoothness, making it to the wall with surprising comfort. Looking around as I made the turn, I was surprised and shocked to see that the other five swimmers (all considerably younger) in the race were well behind me. I pushed off on my back and watched with some dismay as they began to gain on me. The breaststroke was worse, and I touched the wall in fifth place going into the freestyle where I managed to catch up to a couple of the others. Still, I was quite happy mulling over the surprise of my butterfly leg.

That got me thinking that with a little more work maybe, butterfly would be my stroke for the medley relay. By the time the next nationals rolled around, I was ready, substituting the fifty fly for the fifty freestyle. That year I managed third place in the event, completing the two lengths with no difficulty. For a while, however, I still had a problem making the forty-five-plus medley relay because Bill Yorzyk (1956 Olympic gold medalist in the 200 Butterfly) was a club member. He had turned forty-five and was blocking me, but we usually had a B team entered, and three years later, I aged up to the fifty-five-plus team and escaped Bill altogether.

I remember a time when Yorzyk had just turned fifty. We were both standing on the blocks, several swimmers apart, preparing for the start of a five hundred freestyle, an event he didn't generally swim. Bill pointed at me saying, "Look out, Win, I'm in your age-group now!"

Having recently turned fifty-five, I pointed back shouting with a smile of my own: "Bill, you're *never* in my age-group!" There was a good bit of relief in my statement, which was only partially true since relays operate on ten-year age-groups.

I kept working on my butterfly, moving up to the one-hundred-yard and one-hundred-meter events, where over the years I've been quite fortunate, winning many championships and setting national and world age-group records in five age categories. In fact, the one hundred butterfly has been the event where I've found my greatest success in Masters swimming. I've tried the two hundred a couple of times, but whether it's brains or a lack of courage, I'm just not willing to put up with the pain involved in training for the event. If it's the latter, this is a major confession for someone who's supposed to be a distance swimmer, but I take refuge in the thought that my difficulties beyond one hundred yards of butterfly may have something to do with not learning the stroke until I was past fifty.

I truly believe surprises, and especially those that result from being challenged or adventurous, can often provide us with great joy and satisfaction. Such surprises can come in all walks of life, not just from successes in athletics. For me, a dash of the seasoning of adventure adds a wonderful flavor to life. Reaching out and sampling what the world has to offer can lead to a wealth of ideas and accomplishments, a broadened outlook, and the reality of unsuspected talents. The fun, sometimes, is that you usually don't know exactly where the road to adventure will take you. In my case, pushing the envelope a bit made me a butterflyer, opening the door to a lot of success as a Masters swimmer. In another arena, following an unknown road led to an interesting career change. But that's another story, one that has nothing to do with improving your swimming.

Chapter 13

Sidestroke and Other Aberrations

These strokes are all part of swimming, so they need to be covered even if any competitors who read this groan.

To label sidestroke as an aberration is probably unfair. Sidestroke is a perfectly legitimate stroke. In fact, it's a marvelous way to chew up yardage in a relaxed, easygoing style of swimming. Then too, it's a basic lifesaving skill, its "scissors" kick being the engine for most of the propulsion in the cross-chest carry. In the lifeguard trade, the cross-chest carry is seen as the gold-standard technique for rescues that must be made in person without the use of boat or other equipment.

But as a sometime competitor, there's something inside me that makes me see any stroke other than one of the big four (crawl, backstroke, breaststroke, and butterfly) as something lesser—not "real swimming." Yet the sidestroke is important. It's a "resting" stroke that neophyte swimmers can quickly learn since with the swimmer's nose and mouth mostly out of the water, the breathing skills needed are minimal. That's where the resting comes in, when you do your breathing!

Another lifesaving stroke is the inverted breaststroke—also covered in this chapter—a stroke which is actually used successfully by some Masters swimmers in backstroke competition.

Sidestroke Kick

In the sidestroke, the swimmer lies on her side in the water, extending her lower arm forward. The scissors kick is the key to the stroke. The upper leg is extended forward with about forty-five degrees of bend at the knee; the lower leg is extended to the rear also utilizing knee bend. Then the legs are snapped together forcefully. The legs straighten as they are brought together, and there should be a momentary extension. The ankles should remain relaxed.

The sidestroke kick is quite effective, comparable to the drive provided in the breaststroke kick, developing propulsion with less strain on knee or groin, two injury-prone areas for breaststrokers. Some wonder as to whether the upper leg should go forward or to the rear. I've experimented with both, finally opting for upper leg forward simply because that seems less disruptive in the event of a lifesaving rescue where the rescuer is carrying a victim draped on her hip in a cross-chest carry. My advice would be to try it both ways and do whatever feels most comfortable—upper leg forward or upper leg behind.

Sidestroke Arm Action

The arm stroke in the sidestroke is quite benign, and in recent experiments, I found it awkward although I don't remember it being that way fifty years ago when I swam the stroke quite often before becoming a competitive swimmer. The arms do little more than sculling, with the forward arm—the one on the underwater side—pulling backward to the midchest and the opposite (upper arm) pushing the water backward toward the hip from the midchest position where both hands meet.

Sidestroke Timing

The timing in the stroke is a kick, glide, arms, kick, glide, arms sequence. Overall, it's a simple, sedate stroke. Your face is mostly above the surface, eliminating breathing problems, at least in calm waters. If you get the kick right in this stroke, you will have about 80 percent of it down pat. As in breaststroke, you should move your hands and arms to the extended position from the hands-neutral position at the chest with minimal delay. The glide takes place when your arms are extended.

Inverted Breaststroke (Backstroke)

The inverted breaststroke is a form of backstroke utilizing the breaststroke kick (done inverted—faceup) and a double arm stroke. The arms follow the full backstroke pattern although they must describe a shallower path in the water since there is no body roll. The arms recover over the water during the glide phase after the legs have finished kicking and are in the extended position. The timing for the stroke is kick, glide and recover, pull, kick. It is important to hold a long body position in the water, with the arms reaching full extension in front of the head and pulling to a point well below the bottom of the bathing suit before the hands exit the water.

The inverted breaststroke can be a comfortable and effective way to swim. In races of one hundred yards or longer, a number of Masters swimmers have used it quite successfully when competing in backstroke events. The timing is simple—just like regular breaststroke—and breathing is not a problem since your face is always out of the water.

As I suggest earlier in this chapter, the inverted breaststroke has applications in lifesaving. There is a head carry where the victim is towed by the rescuer. In this carry, the rescuer, on his back in the water, cradles the victim's head with both hands and propels himself and victim by kicking. Excessive contact between the rescuer's knees and the victim's back can be a problem in this technique. The closer bond between victim and rescuer provided by the cross-chest carry is more secure. A rescuer who is able to provide a sense of comfort to the victim is doing both a big favor since a sense of security means less panic and a safer rescue.

Trudgen Crawl

The trudgen can be seen as part sidestroke and part front crawl. The swimmer basically swims front crawl with the arms but makes a near ninety-degree roll to the breathing side, executing a sidestroke kick, at the same time breathing. For someone who has not learned correct breathing skills, the relatively long pause in the stroke sequence allows extra time for both exhaling and inhaling. Thus, the trudgen crawl becomes at least a temporary answer for the learner since there's a kind of stalling hitch for breathing in the swimmer's stroke. It's not a thing of beauty, but it allows the swimmer to enjoy himself in the pool. The trudgen can be a way station on the pathway for better swimming, or it can be an end result for decent lap swimming.

It is said that the trudgen crawl was a transition from sidestroke to a more modern way of swimming. The stroke had its heyday in the earlier part of the twentieth century, but now most swim instructors recommend that we learn the proper breathing and kicking skills, thus moving directly to "go"—in this case, real front crawl or in competitive terms: freestyle!

Maybe I'm a bit prejudiced on this subject as a result of being kicked more than once or twice by swimmers using the trudgen. That sidestroke-type kick can reach way out to include the adjoining lane, so watch out if you see a swimmer nearby using the trudgen crawl!

The point of this chapter is to be complete and to offer some suggestions for other ways of swimming. We're not all going to be competitors or even top-drawer lap swimmers. The swimming styles offered in this chapter, like the competitive strokes discussed in earlier chapters, can provide marvelous exercise and the sense of well-being that goes with it.

GOOD SWIMMING

IMAGES AND MOODS

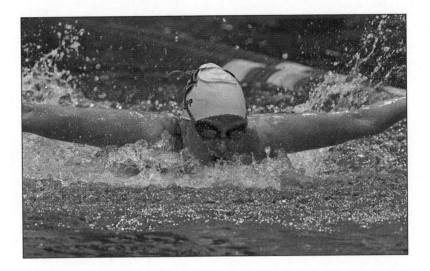

People often ask why this stroke is called butterfly. The photograph above gives us a hint with the arms of world-class swimmer, Julie Stupp, spread like the wings of this delicate insect.

The photography and design on the following pages are by John Forasté. All of the photographs are his, with the exception of the one above and three others that are specifically credited to Peter Bick.

John is a fine swimmer in his own right. His love of the water and swimming comes through loud and clear in the images and moods he has created here for Good Swimming.

The beauty, intensity and technique of the freestyle stroke as seen from both above and below the water's surface.

The sequence below of underwater still images shows the excellent freestyle technique of elite swimmer Mike Lane. These stills are from the *Good Swimming* video. See the last page of the appendix for information on how to order.

Backstrokers have their own special starting method.

Posted workouts and pace clocks are often seen around the pool.

Rich Burrows (Coach to his swimming buddies) working out. He always "mixes it up" with different strokes, drills and time intervals. See samples of his workouts in the first section of the appendix.

Multiple Olympic gold medal winner Ian Crocker shows his strong form in the butterfly.
(Photo by Peter Bick.)

The bottom sequence of stills from the *Good Swimming* video shows elite swimmer Mike Lane demonstrating the butterfly as seen underwater. To order the video, see the last page of the appendix.

Sets of freestyle and kicking on timed intervals are always a part of Coach Burrows' workouts. (Samples are in the first section of the appendix.)

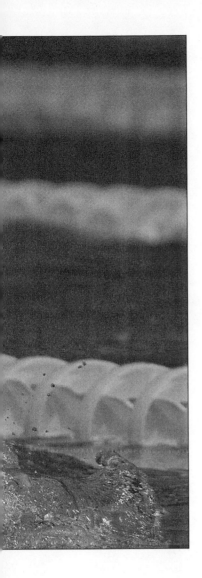

Brendan Hansen, Captain of the 2008 US Olympic Swim team, shows his powerful breaststroke. (Photo by Peter Bick.)

The bottom sequence of stills from the *Good Swimming* video shows Mike Lane demonstrating the breastsroke as seen underwater. To order the video, see the last page of the appendix.

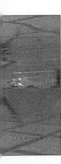

Early morning workouts begin with stretching ...
and waking up.

The anticipation and intensity of competition.

Olympic gold medal winner
Natalie Coughlin in one of
her terrific backstroke starts.
(Photo by Peter Bick.)

The bottom sequence of stills
from the *Good Swimming*
video shows Mike Lane
demonstrating the
backstroke as seen
underwater. To order the
video, see the last page of
the appendix.

wimming is not just an individual sport. Wonderful camaraderie

an be enjoyed in the pool during competition and workouts,

r in the open water sharing a beautiful early morning swim.

Chapter 14

Toys and Other Equipment

This chapter can complicate your life, or perhaps just make it more fun.

Sometimes I feel a lot like Santa Claus. Not in the sense that I'm giving stuff away, but when I go back and forth to the pool, I carry this large mesh sack, chock full of swim equipment. For me, it's pretty essential. There are a couple of bathing suits, a kickboard, two sets of hand paddles (large and small), fins, a couple of pairs of goggles, a pull buoy, my partially inflated rubber inner tube, shampoo, foot powder, and finally, a small box where I keep a razor, earplugs, and bathing cap.

The funny thing about these trappings of the sport: somehow as you stay with it, you think you need more rather than less. There's some pretty fancy stuff you can buy. One of the stellar swimmers in my age-group has a wristwatch that beeps on preset paces. He wears the watch under a bathing cap, even in races, so that he can tell if he's ahead or behind on his intended intervals. We're not all convinced it's really legal, but we let him get away with it.

Then if you really want to go whole hog, you can put in your own lap pool. I don't mean the usual tiny cement-walled, egg-shaped, suburban slough. I mean a real twenty-five-yard one- or two-lane pool where you can work out on pace. I've seen several of these; one in particular, owned by a Masters swimmer friend from California, is especially eye-catching. You walk out on to his back deck and look down into this beautiful two-lane pool, complete with pace clock and backstroke flags. The lane lines are dark blue Spanish tile. It's a marvelous facility. It makes you want to hop off his deck and swim. But then my friend doesn't use it all that much. He tends to work out at the Y with a group.

Down a step from your own lap pool is an "Endless Pool," featuring its own moving current that you swim against. These are contraptions designed for inside use, generally about 10' x 15', filled with water of course, but designed with temperature and current control so that you can swim in place at whatever speed is right for you. The advertisement refers to an underwater mirror for immediate feedback and stroke improvement. It's pricey, definitely a high-end item. Anyone interested can try 800-732-8660. Endless Pool is a trade name, but there are competing products.

More realistically, there's equipment you really do need. First, of course, is a swimsuit. For the regular lap swimmer, I recommend something at the low end of the price range. For working out, I prefer a simple nylon suit. Sometimes, a basic men's suit can be found on sale for under $10. Nylon seems to be increasingly hard to find, however, since most of the manufacturers want to sell you Lycra, a more expensive product that looks better but which tends to wear out more quickly. Lycra is also better for racing since, when new at least, it does create less drag in the water. For men and workouts, the difference in drag is insignificant. The kind of suit I'm talking about is a tight-fitting tank suit, not beach trunks such as seen quite often among neophyte lap swimmers. The advantage of the tank suit is reduced drag and easier swimming in workouts.

Women are not likely to find suits in the $10 range, but then a women's tank suit will not be any more expensive than normal beach wear. The aspect of reduced drag for women is particularly important, and so a correctly designed woman's suit can make a big difference. I remember a professional colleague from Florida I'd encouraged to try Masters swimming who showed up for her event at the National Masters Championships attired in a fetching little number featuring a low neck and some sexy buttons running down the front from the top to about the navel. "Scooping" water inside the front of a woman's suit can be a vexing problem, and the faster you're able to go, the more you're going to scoop. It's like applying the brakes at the same time you're giving it the gas! My friend's suit was fashioned to maximize scoop although I'm sure that wasn't what the designer had in mind.

The better women's suits are designed with high, tight necklines. A snug fit is also strongly suggested. A properly fitted suit, designed to reduce drag, will enable a woman to swim faster than would be possible even in the buff. This was proven a few years ago by some young ladies on a college team who sneaked into their pool at night and tried some time trials both ways—in their racing suits and in the nude. This informal test in its unique way proved a point on the effectiveness of women's modern racing suits.

For the racer, there are some high-end models featuring technical advances for reduced drag. Most of the leading manufacturers are selling these now. Even men are now wearing full body suits made of cutting-edge material, and every year, there's something new on the market. A few years ago, I bought one of these, and I had to agree with my Masters peers that the suit did make a difference in my races, but now my rivals all seem to sport longer and tighter suits made of even more sophisticated material. I suppose I'll have to upgrade to stay competitive.

So now we've got you in a suit. Obviously, you'll need a towel. Once in a great while, I've left my towel at home or in the car. When it happens, I just say to hell with it and go ahead with my workout. This does create problems when it's time to get dressed. Sitting around the locker room waiting to dry is a pain. The paper towels in the locker room just don't cut it. In the old days when I started swimming in college, most pools supplied towels, so we never had to worry about this aspect, and I suppose there may be places left that still extend this nicety, but they're few in number. In addition to a suit and towel, there are some other items of equipment I'd recommend.

Goggles. This is a personal preference item. The most important point for the workout swimmer is leakage, followed in rapid order by comfort, visibility, and price. Style may well be a factor of concern to some. As a competitor, I have to dive in from racing blocks one meter above the water, so it's critically important that my goggles stay on my head, locked in over my eyeballs where they're supposed to be.

Keeping my goggles on during the dive has been something of a problem for me, or at least it was when I first began my latter-day swim career. The flat racing dive I learned in college is slower than the modern, deeper dive competitors now use; and to make matters worse, the flat dive creates forces that pull goggles out of place. Sometimes, they can just fill with water and snapback, causing an element of visionary confusion. At other times, they tend to migrate quickly to the mouth, causing more serious breathing and drag problems. Hence the expression "I ate my goggles on the dive!"

I've finally learned to dive more or less correctly in the modern style and have found a type and make of goggle that seem to work for me. I try to use the same kind of goggles in workouts that I use in races. It's a matter of getting used to something and being comfortable with it, thus avoiding extra worries during the stress of competition.

I still see some people who swim without goggles. I can't understand it. Chlorine and eyes just don't mix that well. I can remember in college, going to the library to study at night after working out a couple of times during the day and seeing rings around the lights and having trouble focusing. This was just the way it was for us; we all saw those rings every night! It was an expectation of the sport. We never used goggles back then, and in fact, they were illegal in amateur competition. Putting goggles on swimmers was one of the key elements that changed the sport since the eye protection they provide make it possible for swimmers to take the longer workouts that have resulted in vastly improved competitive performances. (Another key element resulting in improvement was circle swimming in lanes, which allows more people to use the pool at the same time.)

Goggles open up a whole new visual, underwater element, adding a marvelous dimension to your swimming; and if you do flip turns, goggles become absolutely essential since a much more accurate view of the wall is required for this racing turn.

Folks with vision problems can even buy goggles that include their optical prescription (*C* number). They're not especially expensive and can be ordered through most of the large swim equipment suppliers.

Some people are sensitive to the rubber or neoprene seal. There are goggles that are hypo-allergenic, and then there's that Swedish style with no seal other than the bare plastic rim. Many competitors like these because they're very firm on the dive. I find them uncomfortable.

It's really a question of choice. You need to try out different types until you find something that's right for you. There are goggles that fit over the bone structure surrounding the eye, and there are goggles that fit more nearly inside that bony area, making contact with the softer tissues of the outer eye. You can spend a lot of money for goggles even if you don't need a prescription pair. Happily, I've found that cheaper is better.

Kickboard. Many pools keep these on hand. If you swim regularly at one of these considerate places, you don't need to buy your own. If you do want your own board, there are a number of choices. Some are made of soft material and others hard. Kickboards should be light and buoyant to support the weight of your hands and arms. Most swimmers hold the board using a firm grip at the front, cradling it between their outstretched arms, or even resting their elbows on the board near the sides. In this way, a fair amount of support is provided so that the swimmer can be reasonably relaxed from the waist forward while working out her legs. Kickboards are sometimes offered at the better-sporting goods stores. They also can be ordered through one of the swim equipment suppliers. I've provided some general information on this at the end of the chapter, which should be helpful to anyone wishing to buy swim equipment of any kind.

Swim buoy. The more common type consists of two foam cylinders fastened in parallel by a nylon strap. There are several sizes. This is the item you put between your legs at the crotch to provide buoyancy to the lower body while you practice stroking with your arms—referred to as pulling. The swim buoy is often called the pull buoy for obvious reasons, and it is generally used in conjunction with hand paddles. Many pools will provide buoys.

Hand paddles. These come in an almost endless variety of shapes and sizes. Since hand paddles are an important piece of training equipment, coach/inventors have come up with innovative and sometimes less-than-innovative ideas to cash in on a slice of the market. The objective, I suppose, is to develop the ultimate hand paddle to provide a quick, easy way for the swimmer to develop Tarzan-like arms and shoulders for super swimming. Realistically, we can expect that when properly and consistently used, they will put us somewhere along the road to developing the upper-body power needed for effective swimming. Most of the paddles on the market meet this criterion, so it becomes mostly a matter of personal preference. Size is the paramount consideration. Smaller is better at first. Improper or overuse of hand paddles can cause shoulder-and-elbow injuries. So take it easy and build up distance and speed slowly.

Unfortunately, some pools will not allow the use of this training device. Safety is cited. Paddles, made of hard plastic, usually have fairly sharp edges; and injuries can occur. Be careful.

Probably, the best way to buy hand paddles is to research the matter through a local swim coach or put a call in to one of the numbers provided at the end of this chapter where you can get some advice on what model might be best for you.

Swim bag. Something in which to put all this gear is essential. There are some really good sports bags on the market. I had a pretty nice one, but I kept losing things inside my bag. I finally junked it in favor of a nylon mesh laundry bag. I still lose things momentarily, but there's pretty good visibility from the outside, which helps. It also has two other advantages: it dries out fast, and it was cheap.

Fins. We're now into the category of equipment that is less essential, helpful most likely, but not absolutely necessary to the improving lap swimmer. With fins, once again, there are many choices. Size is a major consideration. I prefer the simple, old, black, rubber type that first came on the market years ago; however, in recent years, there has been a trend toward much smaller, short fins. These do not provide anywhere near the propulsive thrust the large fins give, but they do make you work harder and more nearly mimic the feel of kicking without fins, at the same time giving you the opportunity to work those leg muscles hard. A good way to build up that flutter kick is to practice with both large and small fins as well as with no fins. When you've got the fins on, it's important to kick fast; slow kicking won't do much for you. It's better to kick a length forcefully and rest for a few seconds before doing another length. It's the old interval-training principle of hard work followed by a recovery period.

Tire. This is the small, rubber, partially inflated inner tube I referred to at the beginning of the chapter. This is an item of torture. It is used to create drag to make pulling with buoy and hand paddles more difficult (and less pleasurable). I don't use it much despite the encouragement of some of my fellow swimmers who feel there is considerable training enhancement in the extra resistance it provides. The tube is worn around the ankles after being twisted into a figure eight to form a loop for each foot. Putting the tube on can be a little tricky until you get used to it.

Bathing cap. For some, this is essential. It is for me now. So much swimming over the years has made one of my ears subject to infection, necessitating an earplug on that side. The only guarantee for keeping in the earplug is the bathing cap. But that's just me. Some people like to wear a cap to keep the chlorine out of their hair. Most male and female racers wear caps in competition, since caps do cut down on drag. There are lots of good, reasonably priced caps on the market. In pool situations, *thin* and *cheap* are the watchwords. When I swim in the ocean, I use a thick rubber cap for its insulating quality. We lose a lot of heat from our heads, so for longer swims in cold water (under seventy degrees), the thicker rubber is helpful. On the other hand, for longer races in a pool (eight hundred meters or more), I never wear a cap. I want to avoid heat buildup.

Earplugs. A lot of people use them. I'm clearly not the only person who gets ear infections. There are those made of rubber as well as a soft waxy type. Both work well. Soft earplugs must be molded into shape each time they're used, and after thirty to forty uses, the wax from your ear breaks the material down so that they're difficult to mold. I get my plugs from the drugstore, but swim gear distributors also carry them.

Nose plug. I'm prejudiced against this item. You're supposed to blow air out through your mouth and nose, so using a nose plug makes breathing more difficult. Try to learn to breathe properly. Granted, flip turns create a situation where you're upside down in the water for a split second, and you're under even longer on the backstroke, so it's necessary to learn to blow air out at the critical time you're in this vulnerable position. Most of us learn to do it, but if you find it's too difficult, you do have the option of a nose plug. And there are a few folks with medical situations, usually involving the sinuses, that make the nose plug essential.

Wristwatch. Obviously, this item must be waterproof. It can be used as a pace clock if your pool does not have one. The pace clock is the oversize timepiece with just a second hand (some also have a minute hand) seen around most pools. It's an essential training device for better swimming and building fitness. A watch with a nicely visible sweep second hand will also do the job. Digital watches make good pace-tracking devices as well.

There's a lot more, and this chapter could easily become a book unto itself. There's always plenty of information in the official United States Masters publication: *Swimmer.* This is published every two months and could be of interest to lap swimmers and triathletes as well as registered Masters swimmers.

There are several national distributors of swimming equipment, so my recommendation is to get the magazine and do your shopping by telephone or computer.

Some of the swim equipment distributors include the following:

Speedo	888-477-3336
The Victor	800-356-5132
Kast-A-Way Swimwear	800-543-2763
Toad Hollow Athletics	800-322-8623

Adolph Kiefer & Associates   800-323-4071
Metro Swim Shop Inc.   800-526-8788
Sprint Aquatics   800-235-2156
Nike Swim   800-626-0215
TYR Sport   800-252-7878

This is just a partial list. More information can be found in *Swimmer* and other aquatic publications.

Chapter 15

Finding a Pool (Or Other Place to Swim)

Summers are nice. You don't need a pool if you can find a lake, a river, bay, or ocean. Open-water swimming is especially enjoyable in the hot, hazy days of summer when the cool water is a refresher and not just a medium for exercise. But then even in summer, not all of us are so lucky as to have these outdoor places available.

Folks who live in Florida or the West Coast swim outdoors year-round. Most of their pools are outside, and some are quite large. I always enjoy my winter visits to these warmer climates and the open-air swimming. But on the assumption that there's no nearby ocean or other body of water available, the key then, even in these warm places, is finding the right pool with convenient hours at an affordable price. And location can be an important issue.

For about twelve years, I lived deep in the woods. While wonderfully quiet and scenic, the nearest pools were eighteen miles away. For a Rhode Islander traveling eighteen miles can be tantamount to moving to a new lifetime. Even so, I adjusted, but never relished the long drive and extra hours on the road. I've now moved to town, and while I still miss the country, the city has its good points, and the pools are much nearer.

One day while I was still in the country, my neighbor told me about this wonderful, Olympic-sized pool only four miles away in a motel. I did take a look at it even though the word *Olympic* pushed the needle pretty high on my skepticism meter. The pool was about twenty-five feet long and would not do at all! I don't know how these places get away with calling their oversized bathtubs Olympic-sized anythings! A true Olympic pool has to meet some very strict standards beginning with the fifty-meter length—roughly half the yardage of a football field. Then there are requirements about width, depth, and even the construction of the gutters. Motels just don't have these kinds of pools.

The ideal pool is, of course, an Olympic pool or at least one that's fifty-meters long. Those pools are hard to find, so most of us settle for something less grand. A pool that's twenty-five yards long and has four, six, or eight lanes is just fine. The quality of the water is important. This can vary a lot. Some pools just don't seem to be run very well. The water might be murky, too hot, or too cold. You can find pools that just seem dirty with trash on the bottom or on the deck. And then some places just seem to smell bad or have a scummy look.

Happily, most of the pools, at least around my neck of the woods, are pristine. The water is well tended, and the locker rooms are clean, and happily, most of the time they're not too crowded. Overused facilities can be a problem. It's hard to swim in a crowd, and too many people in a pool lead to unsanitary conditions leading to a high-chlorine level that can be unpleasant.

So you want a clean, well cared for pool, one with water so sparkling and smooth that swimming is indeed a joy. Ask about lane lines. Pools that don't use them tend to be rough. Lane lines also help with crowd control when more than one person will be swimming in the lane. You want to look at the water level. Is it kept right up to the gutter level? Low water means the pool will be rough, and it's also a clue that the pool may not be well maintained.

You now have some information about pools, and you want to do some lap swimming, but you don't have a pool at your fingertips. Where do you start looking? For starters, the local YMCA is a good bet. The Y has a strong tradition in aquatics, and generally, their pools are good places to swim. Some are really great. If you get to Orlando, Florida, check out the Y pool there. It's nearly Olympic and definitely so for length and width. The water's pristine and just the right temperature for training.

Happily for us swimmers, there are YMCAs everywhere. I think there are eleven or twelve in Rhode Island, and I've swum in most of their pools. A Y membership is handy if you travel occasionally. Generally, other Ys will honor your hometown card. The cost of joining is universally reasonable; their pools are usually well maintained although Y water is often kept a little warmer than I like. This is a minor deficit more than made up when I remember there's usually a weight room and other exercise facilities available.

So the YMCA is a good place to start your search. If there's no YMCA in your area, then you've got to look farther. Many colleges have swim teams and good pools and are fairly generous with time allocated for the community. There's generally some kind of fee, and the hours may get you out of bed in the predawn darkness, but it's something to check on. Then there are town pools, community organizations, YWCAs, country clubs, Boys and Girls Clubs of America, health clubs, and high schools. There are even freestanding swim clubs. Above all, don't forget the United States Masters organization. They keep pretty good tabs on where folks can swim, and they will be helpful even if you're not currently interested in joining or competing. Of course, if you are thinking of becoming a competitor, then U.S. Masters membership is a must. The cost is reasonable, and you get a very good magazine, *Swimmer*, access to joining a local Masters club and all kinds of updates and tips that will be helpful to your swimming. In fact, I'd recommend the membership even if competition is not something you're interested in. You'll learn a lot more about your sport. The address is

> USMS National Office
> 655 North Tamiami Trail
> Sarasota, Fl 34236
> Phone 941-256-8767
> Bob Butcher, Executive Director

The Membership Coordinator is a lovely lady named Tracy Grilli, who not only is a very competent swimmer in her own right, but also guaranteed to be helpful. If you call her, say hi for me. She'll be able to direct you to people in your area who can help solve your pool problem.

Chapter 16

The Coach

You could say this is just a story. The story demonstrates rather vividly the importance of a coach, not just for the technicalities of a sport, but also in teaching life skills and the value of relationships.

We used to call him Joe. It was hardly ever Coach. And never Mr. Watmough, even though we all held him in the greatest respect. For me, he was the combination of a college surrogate father and the older brother I never had. He was a big influence on my life.

Pete Brownell, earlier mentioned in this book, introduced me to both Joe and the Brown University pool about three days after I entered the university. Pete, a sophomore, was doing his nice-guy thing, treating his brand-new freshman cousin with kindly hospitality. He knew I liked to swim, so he did the obvious and walked me down to the pool. I was surprised and flattered when the coach called me out of the water, and after introducing himself said, "Wilson, you've got a pretty good stroke. I could use you on the team. How about coming out for practice?"

Until this point, junior lifesaving had been the upper limits of my aquatic know-how. I had learned to swim at an early age under the insistence of a determined mother who strongly and sensibly believed that children living by the sea in the summer ought to be able to swim. Any trauma associated with learning evidently left no lasting scars as I had developed a love and zest for the water, enjoying it best during summer storms when the surf ran strong. It was all good fun for this youthful water rat, but a far cry from the world of competitive swimming.

All this I explained to Joe. "Not to worry," he said. He'd work with me. I didn't really know what I was getting myself into. At first, he had me kicking with a board. The kicking seemed endless. He worked on my breathing. He tinkered with my arm recovery and lengthened my stroke. He had me swim with a rubber inner-tube section, holding my ankles together. About a week into this program, I asked Joe what he had in mind for me. My exact words I think were "What am I going to be, Joe, a sprinter?"

I remember the sinking feeling in my gut that came with his response, "Oh no, you're a distance man! That's your thing—distance. Distance men are real swimmers."

It was a little frightening. I had developed this vision of the 50-yard sprint, of moving through the water with speed and splash, of besting my competition and emerging from the water, quickly and heroically victorious. Still, the coach spoke with confidence about my latent abilities and how I would learn to be a winner over the 220- and 440-yard distances. One of Joe's ever-present qualities was his ability as a salesman. His messages were always delivered with an overlay of confidence. He was very convincing, and I continued my training under his guidance with renewed energy. What I didn't know at the time was that his ranks were thin for these distance events, and he was desperate. Perhaps one of the lessons I might have taken away from this session with Joe, had I known then about his need for a distance man, was that desperation could be the mother of opportunity! I also should have suspected that there was a good bit of con in his personality.

In any case, I progressed. Joe was correct, and I became a pretty good, college middle distance swimmer. I also learned a great deal from Joe, a lot about swimming certainly, but also the lesson of the input/output relationship—the rewards of hard work and also about life and how to get along with people. The pool and Joe's smiling encouragement became the core point for my campus life. I was taking morning workouts and then regular workouts with the team in the afternoon. By today's standards, my daily yardage was far from spectacular. The morning workout was generally twenty-twenty-twenty—meaning twenty lengths swimming, twenty lengths kicking, twenty lengths pulling. On an exceptionally aggressive day, Joe might add another twenty swimming to my regimen.

"What will it be today, Coach?" I'd ask.

"Let's do twenty, twenty, twenty, and twenty," he'd reply with a warm smile. On those "aggressive" days, he'd generally add some bit of coaching advice, such as "Look, Win, I want you to keep it nice and smooth on the twenty-length swims and give it lots of kick."

Even though the distance covered in these workouts was not anywhere near what swimmers do now, it was a good deal by the standards of the late '40s, and I rapidly improved.

As I came to know my teammates, I learned that several others had been recruited in much the same way. The freshman-swimming test was a particularly good venue for Joe to practice his recruiting salesmanship. The test was a one-hundred-yard swim. Those who managed to complete the swim in some form or the other—stop-and-go was permitted—were considered as passed while those who were hopelessly inept ended up in Joe's special swim classes. Joe was fairly generous about passing people, and administering this test put him in a wonderful place to spot team prospects. And every year, he seemed to find one or two.

This kind of recruiting is a far cry from our modern, sophisticated expectations where high school swimmers are wooed, flown in for visits, and made to feel very important and wanted. Of course, this high-pressure recruiting goes on in every sport, not just swimming. Today, the formula for putting together a good team puts a premium on recruiting ability—more so perhaps than on actual coaching and teaching skills. Joe was a pretty good salesman when it came to talking freshmen swim test takers into coming out for the team, but the rest of his recruiting MO was strictly low-key. He was, however, a marvelous teacher, a superb sidewalk psychologist, and overall, a wonderful human being who carried himself with a certain air of humor and understanding, never leaving his concern for the young men on his team far from his thoughts.

Joe came to Brown with an unusual background. Never having completed high school and joining the coaching ranks through a rather humble door, he still managed through the strength of his own intellect and character to have a remarkably successful career. Before becoming a coach, he had been the boiler operator for the Olneyville Boys Club in Providence, but he became interested in swimming, somehow finding time to do some understudy assistant coaching along with his boiler operator duties.

Eventually, a vacancy occurred, and Joe was appointed coach. To be sure, coaching in an inner city, twenty-yard, four-lane boys' club pool during the depression was neither a glamorous nor high-paying position. Joe, however, made the best of it. He developed a number of top-rated swimmers, stars who went on to set national and international records. The Watmough name began to carry a good deal of weight on the local swimming scene, especially since Joe's younger brother, Roy, became a successful coach in his own right at another Providence Boys Club.

When the Brown coaching position became vacant after the death of Coach Leo Barry, Joe was tapped for the position. It was 1946, and he was off and running on a college coaching career that lasted twenty-one years. In those days, swimming was definitely a developing sport. There were a number of icons around the country—Bob Kiphuth at Yale, Matt Mann at Michigan, Mike Peppe at Ohio State to name just three—who were at the vanguard of swimming. Joe's personal guru was Kiphuth who took a strong liking to Brown's personable new coach, opening a number of doors for Joe's professional development, and keeping him posted on what was going on at the cutting edge of the sport. Joe listened and learned, managing to stay technically proficient as a coach despite the shortcomings in his formal education.

And any of those shortcomings were more than made-up in street smarts. With his marvelous people skills, Joe seemed to have a sixth sense about his swimmers, knowing when things were going well and, perhaps more important, when they weren't. Many times he was able to intercede to bail a swimmer out of some jam or, more often, to offer advice on how to avoid one. No doubt in large part due to his interest and closeness to the young men on his teams, swimmers in academic or serious disciplinary trouble were the rare exceptions. Being a good counselor/ombudsman is part of the coaching drill for any competent high school or college coach, and Joe exhibited this marvelous trait in spades.

He had many coaching quirks. One of his pet tricks was to explain some nuance to you and set you off on your own while he retreated to his office just off the pool deck. "Look," he'd say before he left the pool deck, "I want you to press way back with those hands. Make each stroke as long as possible."

Then he would listen to the splashes and, at some critical point, sneak back into the pool area to see how you were doing. Sometimes, he would leave a written note for you when you came in for a morning workout. The implication in the written workout was that Joe would not be there that day. But then after you had started, he would mysteriously show up on the pool deck, stopwatch in hand, ready to berate any swimmer not performing with sufficient energy.

Despite his role as a tough taskmaster, he was always there with a word of praise or encouragement. He must have been a strong believer in the use of surprise as an arrow in his coaching quiver. His team workouts were full of variables. Sometimes, it was swimming across the pool; at other times, there would be endless relays where we would swim a length and get out of the water to walk back to swim again and again and again, or we might do distance work six abreast in a pool with only four lanes. The element of surprise kept things interesting.

"The watch never lies!" was one of his credos. Of course, Joe's interpretation of what the watch said might occasionally shade the truth, depending upon whether he thought the swimmer needed either a dose of coaching optimism or pessimism. You were never quite sure if you'd done some of the times Joe said you'd done after a time trial.

It wasn't always peaches and cream with Joe. Midway through my senior year, he believed my social life was getting in the way of my swimming. I thought I'd been sticking to business, but I was getting very interested in the young lady who was to become my wife, and I may well have been slacking off in the pool just a little. One morning, Joe came down on me really hard: "You're swimming lousy, Win, and I know what the problem is. You're spending too much time chasing around with that girl! You better watch it, or you're going to be in trouble here and with the books too!"

The message was delivered in a gruff, angry tone, not at all in keeping with the friendly, somewhat paternalistic messages I was used to receiving from my coach and friend. There was shock value here. To me, it was as though I'd just been dealt a sudden slap in the face. The "chasing around with that girl," who just happened to be the love of my life, was particularly galling. I remember taking on a quick flare of anger. This was followed by a slow long burn over the next few weeks during which I worked my butt off "just to show that SOB."

After the New England championships, which we won by one point due to our fingernail win in the final relay, Joe apologized, confessing that at the time he was worried he might have overdone his motivating gambits. "I thought you might quit," he said. "I knew we'd need you in the best shape of your life if we had any chance of winning the team championship. I figured I'd have to use you on the final relay (400-yard freestyle) right after your 440, and that's a tough repeat!"

His strategy worked. He motivated me into extra work, and I swam a good one hundred free leg on the relay. Winning the championship meet was a wonderful way to cap off my college swim career. Naturally, I accepted Joe's apology, and we remained good friends after I graduated. His apology and explanation was revealing however. I suddenly realized that my seemingly superbly confident coach was, like most of us, haunted by doubts and fears. I suppose any coach with half a brain will worry about having athletes quit the program. Joe later told me he worried a lot about this, particularly since his swimmers didn't really need to swim to retain any scholarship help they happened to be getting.

Joe liked to relive his coaching experiences, and on one of my postgraduate visits, he told me that what he had seen in my rather crude swimming the day he recruited me was the way I worked my arms in the water. "Those arms!" he told me. "I knew they would develop."

I have often reflected on these comments in the context of Joe's coaching emphasis. Like the cutting-edge coaches of the period, Joe was definitely a leg man. The whole team continually worked on kicking, sometimes almost to the exclusion of other aspects of our sport. It seemed as though we lived on those kickboards! Even though, like most of his coaching peers, he preached kicking back then, Joe evidently recognized that what you did with your arms was key in the sport.

Joe ultimately retired after seeing his handpicked successor installed as coach. He lived into his eighties troubled by the effects of diabetes. He always enjoyed visits from friends and former swimmers who called on him frequently. He loved to chat about swimming, the athletes he had coached, and his coaching philosophy as well as his life at Brown University.

I realize that many readers are basically self-coached, and some of us even prefer it that way. Even so, this vignette highlights by way of personal testimony the value of a good coach. Watmough's teaching and presence was a huge influence on my life in college, and certainly, many younger athletes look to their coaches as role models just as I did. As we move along in life, however, we generally look for something else from our coach. There's help with our technique of course. That's basic, but there are other values that older swimmers are seeking as well.

I've seen some very excellent Masters swimmers, middle-aged or older who are totally coach dependent—even ex-Olympians! They depend on their coaches to outline each workout and look to these coaches for an inordinate amount of support during meets. But I sometimes wonder if some of these swimmers aren't too dependent. Personally, I've always liked to find my own way a little more, not that I don't do some double-checking from time to time with some of the great coaches I know.

The first expectation any of us would have is that a good coach will help us with our technique. That's primero uno! Then too, there's the important issue of support during competition. There's great comfort in having someone in your corner whose support you know you can count on during the sometimes-stressful swim meet experience. It's the same for both younger and older athletes. I definitely understand both sides of this particular question. But then perhaps what some of us are looking for is a sense of liberation so that we can become more self-motivated, develop our own "inner coach," and learn to do it on our own more.

As they put in a few years and become more experienced in life, older athletes need to decide at some point what they want in a coach, but at whatever the desired level of involvement, having a coach to fall back on is a wonderful resource. I'm grateful for having had Watmough during my college days, and then as I think about it, grateful too for the many wonderful men and women whose coaching, tips, and support have helped me to become a better swimmer. My needs and expectations may have changed since college, but I remember the coaches who have helped me over the years with gratitude.

Section 3

Competition

Chapter 17

So You Want to Race

Some more accomplished lap swimmers occasionally want to test their skills in the world of competition. This chapter gives insight and information about Masters swimming and other ways to hone your competitive instincts.

Improvements in swimming are what this book is all about. I've seen several lap swimmers make such leaps ahead that they've entered the competitive arena. It doesn't happen often mainly because most lap swimmers don't generally work out in a way that leads to skill development, but the folks I've seen who've made these strides and become involved in Masters swimming have clearly added a whole new dimension to their lives.

Masters swimming can be described as age-group swimming for the declining years. It's that and a lot more. Founded in 1970 by the late Dr. Ransom Arthur, then Dean, University of Oregon School of Medicine, it's an organized system with its own publication, national office, rulebook, registration procedure, record keeping, and insurance program. Swimmers compete in five-year age-groups starting at age eighteen (eighteen to twenty-four then twenty-five to twenty-nine, thirty to thirty-four, and so on until one hundred and up!).

It's a global organization with world championships every two years. In the United States, we have two national championships annually, short course (twenty-five-yard pool) and long course (fifty-meter pool). There are also races swum and records kept for the twenty-five-meter course, with world records maintained by age-groups and expressed in meters both for the twenty-five-meter short course and fifty-meter long course. American records are kept in yards for the twenty-five-yard (short course) commonly used in the United States.

The YMCA runs its own national championship meets, and at local levels in U.S. Masters competition, there are regional championships and an almost-endless number of smaller meets. So there's plenty of opportunity to exercise your competitive juices in Masters swimming. And if that weren't enough, there's also the Senior Olympics, which breaks out into age-groups starting at age fifty.

Obviously, the world of competitive swimming isn't for everybody. I've seen a number of lap swimmers who would be surefire winners if they entered competition, but they prefer swimming just for enjoyment and the health benefits. More often than I like to admit, I catch myself reflecting on the joys of just swimming for fun without the need to gear up for the pressures of competing, and in fact, for the last few years I've taken the summers off from racing, preferring to swim just for pleasure, mostly in the ocean. That's my own formula for avoiding burnout.

Still, it's amazing to me how many high school and college swimmers just hang up their tank suits after successful racing careers, some even turning their backs on the water altogether. The reality is that many of these people have been competing under some degree of pressure since they were little kids in age-group programs, going on to more pressure as college scholarship athletes in their late teens and early twenties. The burnout is understandable. On the other hand, many former Olympians and college greats have stayed with the sport through the Masters program. Perhaps the wonder is that the dropout rate is not greater.

But Masters swimming is not just for former aquatic stars. The ranks are filled with men and women with very little competitive swim experience. That's one of the great attractions of the program. It's a whole new shuffle and deal, mixing Olympians, college stars, high school swim dropouts, and graduated lap swimmers, for a new competitive venue, where any pressure is basically self-imposed, and generally, your biggest competition is yourself—measuring how you did this time against how you did last month, last year, or even last decade.

My purpose is not to do a sell job for Masters swimming, but rather to present it as a possibility to any lap swimmers who feel both ready and inclined to take the competitive plunge. Again, like the matter of goggles, the type of swimsuit you wear or where you do your swimming, it's all a matter of personal preference. Some folks prefer to compete; others don't. Competition is a challenge that can be made tentatively in graduated small steps at the local level where the competition will be less fierce. So if you think racing might be for you, make the contact and give it a try. If you want more information on Masters swimming, call the national office at 941-256-8767.

If you're considering competition, you'll need to know more about starts and turns. These are critical components for the racer, especially in the sprints where losing seconds or tenths of seconds can make the difference in winning or losing. Some of the next chapters will cover these important matters as well as some tips on better conditioning, training, and even tapering for the big meet you might someday wish to enter.

Chapter 18

David's Story

This vignette introduces some training concepts, showing how they worked for one swimmer.

David is my workout buddy. Or at least he was the last time I looked. The problem is in David I created a monster. There are all kinds of monsters we can produce, and I suppose coaches in all walks of sport give birth to their share. While we may be less anxious to take credit for these creations, we are more than happy to brag about the successes of our swimmers even though good coaching can only be part of the formula for athletic success. More important is the hard work and dedication brought to the equation by the athlete himself.

I'll rush to point out that the monster David and I created together is strictly in the eye of this beholder. And the problem is mine. I can no longer keep up with David in workouts!

I first met David at my pool some ten years ago. He was in his late thirties, overweight and ruled—at least in the water—by a somewhat questionable work ethic. A good deal of his water time was spent in social chatter. Very friendly, he seemed to know everybody. He had been advised by his doctor to try swimming to exercise a bad hip. His motivation was a logical desire to stave off surgery.

We struck up a conversation, and somewhere under David's patina of humor, a solid core of dedication seemed to show through. He asked me to look at his swimming. He was pretty rough with the usual breathing problems and many flaws in his arm action. His legs were more or less useless. Still, David was obviously strong, and his arms showed good latent power. We made some adjustments in his stroke, and he stayed with it.

At first, David was strictly someone I helped when I saw him in the pool. Doing workouts together was out of the question. That changed fairly early in the game, however, after I suggested he get a set of hand paddles and a pull buoy and devote a major portion of his workout to swimming strictly pull sets.

A *set* is a group of shorter exercises completed on a time interval. For instance, a five-hundred-yard set could consist of five one hundred-yard swims, allowing for a thirty-second break between each one hundred. More commonly, the swims would be done on a regular starting interval, perhaps expressed by a coach as "go five one hundreds on two minutes, swim 1:30s!" What that means is the swimmer will do five one hundred-yard swims, trying to maintain a pace close to 1:30 seconds for each swim and will start each of the swims every two minutes. Written out in coaching shorthand, it would be expressed as the following:

5 x 100 yards @ 2:00 minutes—1:30 swim

Sets can be simple or complicated, utilizing swimming distance, resting periods and swim intensity variations throughout the set. In later chapters, we will go into this aspect in greater depth, giving some workout examples, featuring what is commonly referred to as interval training. This is far more effective for conditioning than a total reliance on straight swimming.

I remember working with David back in the early days of his swimming. After some experimentation with easy time trials, we found he was able to repeat fifty-meter swims, using paddles and the buoy on a minute and five seconds. His early workouts expressed in coaching shorthand were variations of as follows:

10 x 50 meters @ 1:05 minutes (pulling)

We wanted him to complete each fifty meters in just under sixty seconds, allowing for a five-second-rest interval. David was able to handle this pace with its short resting interval, and he was very happy with his progress. Soon, we dropped his takeoff times to one minute and then to fifty-five seconds, still with the five-second resting period after each swim in the set. The amount of time you need for the swim is the critical determiner of your progress. With improvement you will find, just as David did, that once you're using a certain starting period, you begin to get more rest because you're actually swimming faster without expending greater effort. As part of the training regimen, you *reward* yourself by using a shorter starting interval, and of course, less rest.

When David went from swims on 1:05 to 1:00, he found he was back to getting only five or six seconds rest again. The same phenomenon occurred when we shortened his starting interval to fifty-five seconds. David found, just as we all do, that his early progress was quite substantial, but that as he began to approach more closely his own physiological limits, improvements came more grudgingly.

But once David was able to do pull sets of fifties on fifty-five seconds, we were able to do some training together. And that was good for both of us. It's difficult to do a lot of solo swimming at training intensity since we tend to give in to the protests of our bodies without the challenge of someone else there beside us involved in the same workout.

I remember when David and I first started training together he would work out on fifty-five seconds while I was doing my sets on fifty, but before long, he was able to drop down to fifty seconds, at least for his pulling. He had some problems getting to the point where his actual swimming was anywhere near as accomplished as his pulling. This is not unusual. Most men and many women find they're able to complete pull sets, using paddles and a buoy, a good deal more efficiently and faster than they can swim. Because of his inexperience and some basic stroke defects, David was an extreme case of this phenomenon. At this early stage in his new athletic career, he swam a lot slower than he pulled. But he was making good progress overall.

Yet as often happens, progress came with setbacks. In David's case, there were elbow-and-shoulder injuries—nothing that sent him to the doctor, but rather, nagging pain that was exacerbated by swimming and especially pulling. These injuries, even though minor, interfered with his training. We both suspect they were caused by mechanical defects in his arm action. David is a very strong man, and he was able to make some pretty good training progress with less than ideal mechanics. Over several years, we've been tinkering with the flow of his arms in the water, working primarily on his tendency to drop his elbows, emphasizing the concept of reaching over a barrel immediately after the catch phase of his pull, and getting his action to conform closer to the more ideal S stroke that the better swimmers typically use.

David's progress has been substantial while mine has been in reverse. There's not a whole lot we can do about the aging process. Until last year, I found I could move ahead of David in training sets when we swam, but once he put on the hand paddles, I was done for! Then more recently, I found he was moving ahead of me when we did unaided swimming. There are a lot of things we can do to train together, but when I claim to have created a "monster," it's simply because the neophyte of a decade ago is now clearly a faster swimmer than his coach!

It's not just that I've gotten that much slower. Something happened to David a couple of summers ago that caused a big change in his arm action. Something clicked for him, and his arms now conform much closer to the ideal. He's had time drops in his training sets over all the distances we generally use. We've also been working on other strokes, particularly backstroke and butterfly, and he's made good progress there as well. And oh yes, he's lost about thirty-five pounds. He does have that tendency to pack weight on when he stays away from the pool for too long a time, but he's far from the roly-poly guy I met a decade ago. A few years ago, he swam in the national one-hour event, coming in somewhere in the middle of the pack in his forty- to forty-four-year age-group, not at all a bad performance considering the short time he had been swimming. He hasn't competed a great deal due to job demands, but he says that's coming.

Whether he does or not is up to him. He's clearly enjoying his swimming more, getting good exercise from it, and finds himself in a very comfortable state of fitness. His hip is doing just fine, and thoughts of an impending operation are no longer paramount. He's also added a strong measure of enjoyment to my own workouts. Most important to me, not only did he become a regular workout buddy, but a good friend as well.

Chapter 19

Basic Anaerobics and Aerobics

If you're serious about your swimming, a little biology will be helpful.
This chapter features some specific physiological information about the
adaptations our bodies make when we work out. Knowledge of some
of the science can be helpful when you design your own workouts.

The classic works on this topic are Maglischo's *Swimming Faster, Swimming Even Faster,* and recently, *Swimming Fastest.* There's some pretty heavy going in his treatment of the subject. It's like working your way through college chemistry texts! I was struck by just how complicated the metabolic process of muscular activity really is. My intention here is to keep it simple, but some of this information is helpful to the fitness swimmer and will serve as a reminder as we seek to make training adaptations. And that's what training is all about—forcing our bodies to adapt and condition for better performance. If you're seeking faster sprint times, you'll do it one way, for faster distance results another.

VO2 Max and the Aerobic System

While the exact chemical process of muscular activity is highly complex, for our purposes, we will remember that oxygen is needed to ensure a continuation of movement. This is basic, and muscular activity occurring as a more or less direct result of oxygen intake is referred to as aerobic. Each of us has our own built-in physiological limit as to the amount of oxygen we can consume and deliver to our muscles. This is referred to as VO2 max, and while training can bring about modest improvement in this innate capacity, it is generally thought of as relatively finite. Maglischo estimates that 10-20 percent improvement is possible. People with a large ability to consume oxygen have a leg up on the endurance events that rely heavily on the aerobic system.

It's fairly simple. An individual with a high VO2 max will have a greater ability to deliver oxygen to his muscles, which will allow more energy to be metabolized aerobically. As muscles are exercised, they produce lactic acid; and until quite recently, physiologists had held that excess lactic acid built-up in muscle tissue under stressful exercise was a critical factor in fatigue or as the athlete might put it, "tightening up."

Lactic Acid as a Fuel

Lactic acid is now more widely seen as a *fuel* for exercise. This modern theory holds that muscle cells under exercise conditions convert glucose or glycogen, which is stored in the muscles as a derivative from food, to lactic acid that is then used as fuel by the mitochondria, sometimes referred to as the energy factories of our muscle cells. In this theory, the phenomenon of tightening up occurs when an athlete under high stress can't metabolize enough oxygen to use all the lactate he has produced as fuel. It is now thought that the tightening up referred to earlier is not from the unused lactic acid itself, but from minute-muscle-cell damage and damage to nearby connective tissues that develop when the athlete's system is unable to burn the lactate. At this point, the athlete has gone over his lactate or anaerobic threshold.

It's a complicated metabolic process, but despite the new knowledge, training methods have remained pretty much the same. Training systems that worked to produce faster runners and swimmers when coaches held the older lactic acid theory still work just fine! While some of the theory may have changed, athletic training has not. Exercise physiologists have learned that the chemistry and physiology of the adaptations our bodies undergo in exercise conditioning are somewhat different than they originally thought.

The Anaerobic Threshold

We have noted that aerobic activity involves the use or burning of oxygen. Anaerobic activity, on the other hand, is movement that takes place that does not require oxygen. Our bodies have two systems that coexist: aerobic and anaerobic. When we swim at a more leisurely pace, within our aerobic capacity (less than VO2 max), we are swimming at an aerobic pace. Once VO2 is exceeded, however, we are working anaerobically.

There are limits, of course, to the exercise we can produce anaerobically, and when those limits are reached, we have arrived at our anaerobic threshold or AT. While our VO2 max is a more or less innate ability where only limited improvements can be effected, proper training can result in tremendous advances in AT. It is therefore generally thought that conditioning aimed at improving AT is the most effective route toward better middle distance and distance performances by athletes. Even so, anaerobic training will also improve a swimmer's VO2 max to some degree, primarily by developing efficiencies in cardiac stroke volume and output as well as in circulatory and muscle cell adaptations, making for more efficient oxygen consumption.

AT is enhanced through training primarily by increasing the rate the body is able to use lactate as fuel. The physical changes that occur include greater muscular efficiency, much of which occurs as the mitochondria in the muscle cells themselves increase in mass and thus are able to handle greater amounts of oxygen. Intense training is seen as the most effective method for building mitochondria mass making them more efficient, and thus allowing them to metabolize more oxygen and burn more lactate to enable the muscles to work longer and harder. Another positive physical change provided by training is an increase in the number of enzymes used in glycolysis, the breakdown of glycogen in the muscles that help to fuel our energy systems.

The Immediate Energy System

Just to make it a little more complicated, we should note that our bodies also have an immediate energy system, largely independent from the other two systems, aerobic and anaerobic. The immediate system will provide us with athletic activity for several seconds at the beginning of a race before either of the other systems kick in. This can be noticed by a swimmer in the first few seconds of an all-out sprint race, such as the fifty-yard freestyle or even in longer races. The feeling is one of getting a "free ride." You're swimming hard but at no physical cost. Of course, it doesn't last long, and then you've got to go to work.

While the effect of the immediate energy system is short-lived, with recovery, it will recharge. Typically, a well-trained swimmer will be able to call on this system in a longer race during the push off after each turn. Remember it's flip, push off, glide, and kick. During the push off itself and the hard kicking after the glide, there should be a benefit from this immediate system.

Then too despite the seemingly distinct descriptions in this chapter of these three energy systems, there are no clear lines either between the aerobic and anaerobic systems or the immediate system described here. The demarcations tend to blur. A swimmer, whether racing or training, is always using all three. There can be a great deal of shifting back and forth among them. It's more a question of relativity. In a longer race, it's mostly aerobic and in a sprint, mostly anaerobic.

How It Works When We Train

VO2 max and AT are interrelated. As we develop our capability to consume more oxygen (improved VO2 max) at higher workloads, we also become more efficient at lower than maximum efforts. With this efficiency, our muscular activity will produce lesser amounts of lactate. Likewise, when we are able to increase our ability to metabolize more lactate and oxygen, our systems work more effectively for better athletic performances.

Modern training methods tend to develop both the anaerobic and aerobic systems. Generally, for the lap swimmer—and of course for triathletes and other competitors too—breaking the distance to be swum for the day into shorter increments of fifty to one hundred yards, maintaining a somewhat faster pace than ordinarily swum for the distance, and allowing a resting period of five to fifteen seconds between increments, will develop these systems better than a steady diet of unbroken swimming. By swimming at a faster than usual pace, extra stress is placed on aspects of both the anaerobic and aerobic systems. The short-rest period allows for recovery, and the truly magical part of this is the resulting physical adaptations our bodies make to the extra stress. These adaptations occur relatively quickly and can be measured over weeks and even days. Recovery is an important ingredient in the process where our bodies make adaptations during training. It can be described simply as a cycle: stress, recovery, improvement. This is the training effect. Subsequent chapters enlarge upon this concept in detail to provide specific training suggestions.

Fast Twitch and Slow Twitch

It may not make that much difference to the fitness swimmer whose long-term goal is better health, but it's worth noting that all of us are different in our muscular makeup. There are two basic types of muscle fibers—fast twitch and slow twitch. Fast-twitch muscle will contract more rapidly than slow twitch. Fast-twitch muscles provide power and speed but have less staying power while slow-twitch muscle fibers have less power but are good for a longer duration. Each of us has a combination of the two types in our muscular systems. Those whose systems are comprised to a greater degree of fast twitch will be blessed with speed—in other words, sprint types. Fast-twitch muscle fibers perform well anaerobically for quick bursts of strength. Athletes with a preponderance of slow-twitch muscle fibers will likely have less all-out speed but will have talents as distance athletes. Slow-twitch muscle fibers metabolize oxygen more efficiently for aerobic performance.

Short of submitting to a muscle biopsy, it's not possible to learn exactly the composition of our muscle type although correlations have been found by testing basic athletic skills such as vertical jump. Athletes who can jump the highest will likely have the greatest number of fast-twitch fibers and will therefore more likely be expected to find their best success as sprinters.

This is, of course, a gross oversimplification of the subject. There are, for instance, subtypes of muscle fibers, and then it is thought that training itself can actually effect changes in the basic makeup of our muscle fiber distribution. Thus a heavy dose of distance training for an individual with a high preponderance of white, fast-twitch muscle fibers will, over time, cause some of the fast-twitch muscle fiber to convert to red, slow-twitch fibers, leading to improvements in VO2 max. The reverse is also true with conversion possible from slow twitch to fast twitch, resulting in greater sprint speed and AT. The body is indeed capable of marvelous adaptations.

Still, while these kinds of changes and adaptations are possible, generally we are more likely to have success when we go with the flow and when blessed with a certain kind of muscular system or certain kind of body, try to stay within the limits nature has assigned for us when we seek to develop athletic skills. The "drop-dead" sprinter, trying to become a professional marathon swimmer, is going to be over his head. The swimmer who can only do an eight-inch vertical jump will not be a candidate for records in the fifty-yard freestyle!

Unless we're coaches or exercise physiologists, we really don't need a lot of in-depth knowledge about aerobics, anaerobics, and muscle fibers. It's helpful, however, for the lap swimmer or the competitor to have a little basic knowledge, not only for workout planning, but also for self-assessment.

Self-knowledge can lead to more realistic expectations. If, for instance, you are a budding fitness swimmer, but in your self-analysis you find you have a thirty-inch vertical jump and reasonable overall athletic skills, you might want to approach your swimming somewhat differently than if you could only jump half so high. In the former instance, while your natural VO2 max could likely be lower, the high vertical jump suggests the possibility of developing your swimming rather rapidly and becoming a sprinter in the Masters program. If you preferred not to compete, but rather to swim for fitness, you would recognize that your swimming skills, stamina, and speed over a long distance might come more grudgingly than they would to someone whose vertical jump was only half yours, but who, in all likelihood, would have a better-than-average VO2 max.

Happily, most of us seem to have bodies whose muscular makeup and talents are a blend of both types. In other words, generally, we are blessed with systems that will lend themselves both to speed and endurance when trained. We may not have the blazing speed of an Alexander Popov, the great Russian sprinter, or the endurance of a Lynne Cox, whose extreme swims include all the usual channels, plus the Bering Strait and Antarctica. Nevertheless, most of us, with proper training, can learn to do acceptably in either the sprint or distance venues. Again, I would suggest doing some basic self-analysis to determine in which direction—sprint or distance—nature has aimed you. Self-analysis can help us shape our objectives and keep our goals realistic.

You may wish to try the vertical jump as part of your own self-analysis. It's quite simple. Find a wall where you can jump. Reach as high as possible, standing on your toes. Mark the highest spot you can reach; and then without running, jump, marking the height of your jumping touch. The difference in the two marks will tell you how many inches you are able to jump. It's difficult to suggest what a "normal" or average vertical jump is. Much depends on the height and age of the athlete. Forty inches or more would get you close to the maximum while five or six inches would be the low-end of the scale. Somewhere between a foot and two would be about average. And remember, this is just a starting point in determining whether you are more naturally a sprinter or distance type.

If you want more information on sports physiology as it pertains to swimming, I definitely recommend Ernest Maglischo's books—*Swimming Faster, Swimming Even Faster,* and most recently, *Swimming Fastest.*

Chapter 20

Training: The Clock Is Your Friend

This chapter gets us right to the heart of things—how to train more effectively. The chapter is written primarily for the lap swimmer who's looking for a more challenging and effective workout even perhaps with racing in mind. Triathletes and other experienced competitors may pick up a few ideas as well.

The clock I'm referring to is that peculiar item on the wall or side of your pool somewhere, the one with the endless second hand that goes around and around, never telling what time it is. Believe it or not, this clock is one of the key instruments leading to better swimming and physical training. Oddly enough, most lap swimmers don't seem to know how to use it or, perhaps, even what it is.

The clock truly is your friend. It has countless uses. It can keep you in the groove for a slow, easy workout, or it can to be a fiendish, cruel taskmaster, whipping you along as you put yourself through a regimen of painful "quality" training sets. I tend to see the clock as my friend because it is my reliable helper as I seek to condition. It adds an element of interest and precision to what would otherwise be the drudgery of just getting in and swimming for a certain distance or certain amount of time. It is very easy to lose track of what you're doing if you don't have an objective measure. Without the clock, progress can become subject to feelings of misplaced optimism or victimized by the pain threshold. The pace clock gives you the ability to break your workout up into smaller, more effective increments. It adds a sense of awareness and challenge to what you're doing.

Most lap swimmers are in effect fitness swimmers. They're in the pool exercising because they want to attain a certain level of physical conditioning. Presumably for most of us, this includes weight control and the various aspects of circulation, heart and lung metabolism as well as muscular strength and flexibility. Swimming is good for all of this, but some approaches to your workouts will be more effective than others. And that's what the clock is all about.

Interval Training

The interval-training concept has already been introduced in an earlier chapter, "David's Story," and it is critical to making solid conditioning gains. Interval training features a series of swims of a certain distance completed on specific time intervals. The series of swims is referred to as a set, and the swims within the set are called repeats. While the long, easy swimming done by most lap swimmers may tune the heart and vascular system to a degree, exercise physiologists have shown that for this as well as for building muscle and controlling weight, interval training is far more effective. So if it's better for you, will make you learn to swim faster, and is also a more interesting way to exercise, why don't more lap swimmers do intervals? Probably the answer is that most just don't understand the joys and benefits of doing it with the clock.

The ways you can do interval training are endless. There are repeats at various distances done at a steady pace, descending repeats where you try to complete each swim in the set at a somewhat faster pace than the one before, repeats where you shorten or lengthen the time interval between swims, "ladders," where you do progressively longer swims within the set, topping out at some specific distance and then do progressively shorter swims, adjusting the time interval based on the length of each repeat within the set. These are just some of the possibilities. You can keep it simple or dream up complexities as you design your own interval program.

Generally, I like to keep things simple. I do a lot of short swims, typically fifties and one hundreds on set paces. When I'm in serious distance training, I substitute these with longer swims (five hundreds or even one thousands) once a week or so. Nevertheless, for me the longer stuff takes a certain amount of discipline. The shorter swims somehow are more fun—at least to my way of thinking. My typical workout in a twenty-five- or fifty-meter pool might consist of:

300-400 meters easy swimming
20 x 50 meters at 0:55 seconds (start every 55 seconds)
200 meters kicking with fins
200 meters backstroke with fins
4 x 50 meters fly at 1:30 (start every minute and a half)
200 meters kick (no fins, some sprint kicking)
20 x 50 meters at 0:50 pulling (paddles and buoy)
Go easy for the last four repeats for warm down

This workout would get me to 3,100-3,200 meters or about what I do when I'm in the more intensive phases of preparation for a major Masters meet like a national or world championship. To be honest, it's a good deal more than I enjoy doing. My level for pleasure is about two thousand meters done four days a week. In the pool, it might look like:

300-400 meters warm-up, easy swimming
12 x 50 meters at 0:55 seconds
200 meters fin kicking
100 meters backstroke with fins
4 x 25 meters fly with fins at 0:35 seconds
100 meters kick
12 x 50 meters pull at 0:55 seconds

This latter type of workout is enough to keep me reasonably fit, but not enough to put me into the kind of condition necessary for national competition. There are a couple of men in my age-group who do more than five thousand yards a day, much of it high-quality work. One competitor, a backstroker in his late sixties, suddenly started to excel in the distance events. His secret was doing four thousand yards in the morning, taking a noontime nap at home, and then going back to the pool for another four thousand yards! That amounts to building your whole life around swimming, and I can't help but wonder if that amount of intensive exercise is good for us old codgers.

But where does all this leave the lap swimmer who's into this primarily for fitness? The answer lies within each of us. We must determine what our particular goals are and act accordingly. Most lap swimmers I know are working out for health purposes, and although most of them don't talk about it much, it's clear from my discussions that many of them would like to see improvement in their swimming. To accomplish this, they need to go after their conditioning a little more seriously, in much the same way competitive distance swimmers practice, only somewhat less intensively.

In the lingo of coaches and competitors, this would involve repeats of various distances with short intervals between the repeats. For the lap swimmer who likes to do her mile every morning in a twenty-five-yard pool, my suggestion is to break the mile up into segments. A swimmer who does that mile in forty minutes is swimming at a pace of approximately two minutes and thirteen seconds per one hundred yards, figuring eighteen by one hundred yards to the mile. For improvement and better conditioning, what this swimmer should do is swim a set of eighteen by one hundred yards as follows:

18 x 100 yards at 2:20 (start every 2 minutes and 20 seconds)

This long set would allow the swimmer to move at approximately two minutes and ten seconds pace, just a little faster than her usual pace for the distance, and take ten seconds rest between repeats. Or perhaps more effectively, the workout could be broken down as follows:

6 x 100 yards at 2:20—repeat set three times

In this workout, the swimmer would try to swim the one hundred-yard repeats at a two-minute pace and would therefore earn a twenty-second-rest break between each swim. A two or even three-minute break would be taken between each set. As a result, the "fitness swimmer" is now putting a little more stress on her cardiovascular system and demanding a little more of her body in the workout, even though the distance swum has remained the same. Swimmers who work out this way quickly find they're able to swim the individual distances (repeats) at a faster pace. They then are able to cut back on the starting times of each repeat. The two minutes twenty seconds starting times might drop to 2:15 or 2:10 within a week or two. Obviously, if you're swimming faster and more easily, you're improving. The clock then becomes the tool by which you can measure your improvement and the state of your conditioning.

It's important to vary the distances you swim in repeats each day. You avoid getting into a rut this way, and you will more effectively train your cardiovascular system as well as your muscles. One day, you might swim two sets of four two hundred-yard swims.

4 x 200 yards at 5:10 (repeat twice with three-minute rest)

Of course, this would only get you to 1,600 yards total, but you could either reward yourself by taking a shorter workout or do a few fifty yard swims to warm down. Or you could break your work up into much shorter increments. I do a lot of swimming using fifty yards or fifty meters as my repeat distance. The mile broken up into fifties might look like this:

10 x 50 yards at 1:10 (swim pace 1 minute—1:05)

Repeat the set three times plus three hundred yard warm down.

All of the interval workouts I have suggested here revolve around the swimmer who can do the mile in forty minutes. This is a decent time for a middle-aged lap swimmer, but not everyone swims it this fast, and a few swim it faster.

Your workout needs to be adjusted to take into account where you are on the speed scale. This involves the clock. One way to find out how fast you should be swimming the mile, or at least to set a reasonable pace for your own ability, is to time yourself for fifty yards swimming at your usual pace. Then try another fifty swimming just a little faster. These two swims should give you a pretty good idea of the kind of goal times you need as you break your workout into the smaller increments.

The idea is to do ten or so fifties with a five- or ten-second rest period between each swim. Whatever pace and interval you find workable for fifties can be doubled (both swim time and resting time) as you program your workout for one hundreds, doubling again for two hundreds. The beauty of this workout system is that you can measure quite accurately the improvements you'll make over days and weeks as you find yourself taking less time to complete the repeats. The improvements will come because you're becoming better conditioned and, perhaps, because you're beginning to swim more efficiently. This kind of workout will guarantee better conditioning. Greater swimming efficiencies may come about through a combination of putting more stress on your system and through some of the stroke hints found elsewhere in this book.

Warm Ups and Warm Downs

Warming up and warming down are important. I've found warming up is more critical these days than it was years ago—or maybe it's just that I'm more in tune with what I'm doing. I find now that I need at least three hundred yards of swimming before my muscles warm up and I'm able to swim efficiently. It shows on the clock. When I start swimming a set without a warm up, the first few repeats don't feel right, and they're significantly slower than the ones I'll do after I get that first three hundred yards behind me.

Warm downs can also be important especially if you've done a lot of hard, anaerobic swimming. Some slow, easy swimming at the end of your workout will help stabilize your muscles and reduce the likelihood of stiffness. Basically, the harder your workout, the more you should pay attention to doing two hundred to three hundred yards of easy swimming as a warm down.

Anaerobic Swimming for Improvement

It doesn't make sense to try to do a lot of anaerobic work if you're swimming for pleasure and general toning. Having said that, however, we need to remember that coaches universally have accepted the idea that anaerobic training is critically important to good conditioning among competitive swimmers. Faster lap swimmers may want to take heed to this point for further improvements. A faster lap swimmer might be defined as a swimmer—male or female—who can complete the mile in around thirty minutes. Again, considering the mile as 1,800 yards, the swimmer who can do a mile in thirty minutes is swimming at a pace of one minute and forty seconds per one hundred yards. Some anaerobic training programmed around this pace might look like:

    300 yard easy swim warm up
    5 x 100 yards at 4 minutes (swim each repeat 1:30 or better)
    300 yard swim (normal-mile pace)
    5 x 100 yards at 5 minutes (swim each repeat 1:20 or better)
    200 yard easy swim warm down

This type of workout will create greater physical stress of the kind that will encourage quicker training adaptations resulting in faster, more efficient swimming and better conditioning. How much below 1:20 the swimmer is able to go in swimming these repeats, and what effort is expended will give clues to the swimmer or coach as where the swimmer's anaerobic threshold actually is.

And this—high-quality, long-rest swimming—is only one kind of anaerobic training. There's also race-pace training where you break a race into race-pace goal increments, swim on the pace you select, and use short five- to ten-second rests after the repeats. There's also an all-out sprint training where you go fifties or even twenty-fives with good rest (at least two minutes for the fifties and one minute for the twenty-fives). But generally, I don't see the need for most lap swimmers to do a lot of this kind of training. It can be quite painful. For serious triathletes and other competitors, some anaerobic training is a must.

It's clear, however, that lap swimmers can reap the benefits of modern interval training to achieve better conditioning. That's what the clock is there for. So consider it your friend even though it won't always seem so friendly if you pick paces that are too fast for you. But keep at it; you will improve!

Peaking and Tapering

Part of the planning a serious competitor does heading into a major championship meet is the taper. Tapering is a period of controlled backing off after several weeks or months of intensive training. For the racer, the intensive training period peaks about three weeks prior to the meet. Then the competitor goes into the taper period, gradually reducing yardage and intensity as the meet approaches. Tapering allows the body to rest and recover and sharpens the swimmer for the major event he's been pointing toward. This is something most lap swimmers don't have to worry about, but triathletes and other long distance competitors need to do some tapering even if it's only for a few days prior to their event. Tapering for a distance event is generally much shorter than the three weeks mentioned above, but each of us must find out what works for us individually. I've found, for instance, that for a two-mile open-water swim, a six-day taper works just fine for me.

Tapering is tricky. You can overdo it and come out flat for your meet or event, or you can cut it too short and not maximize the rest you need. A problem, which I call the taper doldrums, often arises during the second week of a taper. You find your swimming is way off, you feel uncoordinated in the water, and you worry that you've blown it. But then in the third week, you usually pull out of it and start feeling very strong and swimming well; however, if the taper is cut too short, swimmers can often check in for their meet still in the period of doldrums. Tapering is highly individual. What works for one will not necessarily work for another. In planning for a taper, it's critical to pay close attention to the conditioning work that has been done during the training and peaking period prior to the taper.

Building Up after a Layoff

While tapering may not be an issue for most lap swimmers, they and competitors alike should take heed to the need to build up gradually after a layoff. You definitely lose it quicker than you get it back! And the older you are, the faster you lose it and the harder it is to get going again. So there's a need for patience in the process. Building up is fairly simple. You just do what feels right the first day and then try to do a little more the next day although quite often the second and third days after a layoff can be the most challenging. So don't expect to increase your yardage or quality of your workouts too quickly.

When I allude here to the quality of your workout, I've assumed that by now you're convinced that the way to go is interval swimming. Try it; you'll enjoy it! It clearly is the formula for improvement. If you set a goal to improve with specific targets and a plan to reach that goal, surely you will improve.

Chapter 21

Starts

If you are or want to become a racer, this chapter should be helpful. On the other hand, maybe you're a fitness swimmer looking to spice up your workouts with a flashier beginning. A good start will fill that bill!

Typically, lap swimmers ease themselves into the water, sometimes utilizing a ladder or even stairs, leading to the shallow end. Then there is some maneuvering to a lane and the wall, a push off and on to swimming. There's no need to dive. In fact, some pools even regulate against diving. Where I generally swim, they cordon off the starting blocks, but I can and do dive in from one end as I start my workout. I like to dive right in because it reminds me to start correctly, keeping my goggles on.

But if you do indeed want to race, you should know how to start. I suppose this is not an absolute since the Masters rules are pretty liberal on this. You're allowed to start from the side of the pool, either in the water or from the edge, as well as taking off from the blocks. Realistically, in a distance freestyle race, starting from the side of the pool is not a terrible handicap, but in shorter races—especially for those fifty-yard dash events—the body length or so you lose from the in-the-water start is critical.

Starting in the Water

In local meets, we see quite a few folks starting from the water or from the end of the pool rather than from the blocks. Starting in the water is simple. You just hold on to the side of the pool; and when the starter gives the signal, you push off, glide for as long as you can underwater, pick up your kick as you move to the surface, and start stroking. Generally, it's our newer competitors who have not yet learned how to keep their goggles on while diving that opt for the in-the-water start. As in so many things, there's a trick to keeping your goggles where they're supposed to be when diving in.

Keeping the Goggles On

Learning to keep those goggles on is the first focus in learning to start properly. Start by finding a pair you like and getting the strap nice and tight. A smaller pair of goggles that fit underneath the bones of the eye socket will be more forgiving when you dive. As you adjust your goggles, you should be able to feel a sense of vacuum when you press them against the soft tissue around your eyes. Most swimmers like to fiddle with their goggles as they prepare for the race, making infinitesimal adjustments and testing them for the proper suction. Keeping them on is a function of finding a pair that fits well, providing some suction around the eyes, and learning to start correctly.

And the Start Itself

It's best to start the learning process from the deck at the deep end of the pool, forgoing the blocks and their one-meter height above the water. At the deep end, stand facing the water with your toes curled over the edge, flex your knees a little, and go for it. Be sure there is at least six feet of water when you're starting because you're probably going to go a little deeper at first. As you dive, stretch your arms out in front of your head so that they will break the surface of the water for you. Duck your head and plan to go in fairly deep for your first dive. The key is ducking your head just as you enter the water. Once you're under the surface, bring your head and arms up again, get your kick going, and start stroking as you break out into the air. Some people are able to keep their goggles on right from the beginning; others—like me—need to try and try again until they get it.

Once you're able to keep the goggles on diving from the pool deck, it's time to try it from the blocks. Things will look somewhat ominous until you get used to the one-meter height. The dive is just the same as described in the previous paragraph. One tip that seems to help is to think of going into a hole as you dive. The hole starts with your hands then your head, chest, lower body, and legs all flow right into the hole. Once you've got it down with a low-powered dive, you can begin to apply more leg drive, with the objective of making that hole farther away from the blocks. Head position is all-important. The rest of your body will follow the lead of your head.

It may take a long time for you to get used to keeping your goggles on as you make these dives. It's a question of repeated practice to make it happen. Believe me it will, provided you're using goggles that fit properly and are suitable for diving. A small confession here. It took me about five years into my Masters comeback before I found the right combination of technique and goggle type so that I could dive with some degree of confidence. I still worry about it.

The Grab Start

Now that you're able to keep your goggles on, you can learn the kind of starts competitors use. The grab start has been the most common. You flex your knees and reach down to grasp the block, either between or outside of your feet. This is a matter of personal preference. Lean slightly forward. When the starter's horn or gun goes off, press your hands forward and launch yourself off the block. Remember that hole you want to enter: hands, head, chest, lower body, and legs all flowing into the hole you made with your hands.

Breaststrokers will go somewhat deeper than freestylers and butterflyers in order to take advantage of the full underwater pullout and kick. Butterflyers who use an extended underwater dolphin will also dive more deeply. How far you should try to stay beneath the surface after your dive is an individual matter that needs experimentation and technique refinements. Swimmers with great kicks can benefit by staying under longer. Swimmers who have weaker kicks need to get to the surface more quickly. The action you take after entering the water is basically the same as the glide, stroke, and kick sequence described in the chapter on turns. Remember to stretch out—streamlined!

The Track Start

We're seeing more swimmers today using the "track start." In the track start, the swimmer grasps the blocks by the outside corners or wherever it's comfortable at the front, keeps one foot also at the front, but draws the other leg back toward the rear of the block. When the starter says, "Take your marks," the swimmer rocks backward. When the gun or horn sounds, the swimmer pulls hard with both arms at the same time driving forward with his legs. The arms go forward and the same sequence as outlined for the grab start occurs with the swimmer entering the water through the "hole" made by the hands. Some swimmers who do the track start well believe it provides an infinitesimal edge, not so much that it provides a quicker getaway, but because the additional thrust generated by bringing the arms into play seems to place them slightly farther out in the pool when they enter the water. Other swimmers are sticking with the grab start, so any difference is infinitesimal.

The Backstroke Start

Backstrokers have their own unique way of starting. At the signal from the referee, backstrokers will enter the water and swim back to the blocks. A backstroker starts with her feet on the wall and pulls herself into a crouched position using the bar under the block. The rules stipulate that the swimmer's feet must be on the wall rather than curled over the gutter. Since it is tiring to hold yourself in the crouch, swimmers ordinarily do not pull themselves into this position until the starter says, "Take your mark."

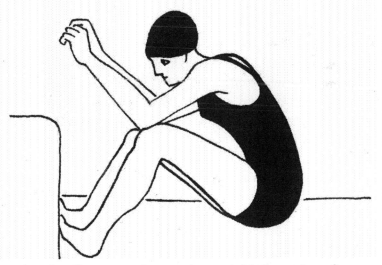

Backstroke. Illustration shows swimmer initiating action of start by letting go of the starting block and thrusting with the legs.

When the horn or gun goes off, the swimmer will throw her arms back at the same time driving with her legs. The back is arched, and the swimmer clears the surface in a good backstroke start. Once again, the swimmer will try to enter a hole in the water with her body. This backstroke start is quite explosive and athletic. It demands good leg power. Any of us can push off and fall back into the water, but we lose a lot of ground to those who do the start well.

Backstroke. Illustration shows swimmer in full flight after start with nice arch for clean water entry.

Dolphin Kicking Underwater

Many of the top backstrokers are now doing an extended upside-down dolphin kick on starts and turns, taking advantage of the fifteen yards (fifteen meters in pools of twenty-five or fifty meters in length) allowed in competition. Those blessed with this kind of kicking ability have a solid advantage over those who don't. Good kickers are able to accelerate rapidly and drive themselves to the surface to begin stroking with strong momentum. Butterflyers and even some freestylers who have good dolphin kicks are now also doing the extended kicking underwater on starts and turns, finding it a faster way of propulsion than swimming on the surface. Swimmers who do not have this great kicking ability do the same glide, kick, and then after driving to the surface with somewhat less kicking and momentum, start their stroking. For backstrokers, the pattern is similar to freestyle or butterfly except swimmers must be on their backs during this underwater phase. This, again, is just the same as the push off sequence on turns.

Stretching It Out and Being Quick

In all starts, just as in the case of turns, swimmers should stretch out in a streamlined position during the glide and as the kick begins. Holding this lengthened position in the water will pick up extra distance in the glide-and-kick phase. Another tip is to listen to the starter and be ready—on a hair trigger—to take off when the horn or gun sounds. Quick starts are especially important in the sprint events. Swimming races can be won or lost by inches or fractions of seconds. So learn to go at the sound of the horn. Hone those reflexes and learn to be athletic on your starts.

Illustration shows good stretched out form after turn, all strokes (backstroke inverted)

Chapter 22

The Day I Ate My Goggles

I suppose this chapter could be titled Learning from Adversity. That's what it's really all about. It's sort of a first-person parable involving several swimming and life lessons.

The truth is, I've eaten my goggles a number of times, but this was really bad. Learning to dive properly so that the darn things stay on had been a major accomplishment for me. All of us who began to swim competitively back in the forties and fifties had the same problem.

We were taught to dive flat. In competitive swimming's infancy, that's what a "racing dive" was—a flat dive where you drove hard with your legs and hit the water with a glancing blow, mostly on your chest. My coach even went so far as to string a clothesline across the pool we were supposed to clear and still hit the water with a flat, skidding dive. It wasn't until much later that the experts realized they'd been wrong, discovering a deep dive was actually faster. In the deeper dives of modern racing technique, you meet the water more gently and are able to generate more thrust with your legs after you enter; whereas the flat dive, with its quite violent and extended entry, creates a greater area of friction against the water, slowing the swimmer.

An important by-product of the modern, deep, racing dive is that your goggles are far more likely to stay on. The gentler entry, plus the fact that your face is shielded by the top of your head and arms as you enter through the hole your hands create, makes keeping those goggles where they're supposed to be a realistic expectation. The problem a lot of us older folks had was not so much learning the new way of diving, but rather one of regression. The heat of competition would make us go on automatic, and we'd dive the way we were originally taught—hard and flat.

During my several-year learning period, all kinds of problems occurred. Sometimes, I'd get lucky; and the goggles would just flip up, fill with water, and come back down where they were supposed to be. If I was really lucky, maybe only one eyepiece would fill up. Swimming a long freestyle race with its many flip turns could be quite interesting with water-filled goggles. It was even more interesting and definitely frustrating when, as a result of an especially vigorous dive, they'd end up somewhere else on my face.

I think several of us on the New England Masters team actually compounded our problems when, instead of concentrating more thoroughly on learning the new diving technique, we played around with our equipment. We were using a Speedo goggle that fitted around the eye socket. It's a comfortable goggle and still quite popular. We widened the strap-attachment slots and substituted a heavy gauge inner-tube section for the factory-issue strap and then adjusted the fit so that our goggles were worn painfully tight. Most of the time, we were able to dive flat, and they'd stay on. But not always.

The day in question happened during my fourth Long Course National Championships. I had become a factor in the one hundred butterfly and felt I should win the race even though I had to confront a younger competitor named Hal Begal who had just "aged up." Hal was an exceptionally fast sprinter both in freestyle and butterfly. Pretty much conceding the one hundred freestyle to Hal, who was a true-speed demon in the sprint freestyle events, I'd been pointing toward the one hundred butterfly, which I was beginning to regard with a sense of ownership. In the weeks leading up to the meet, preparation for it had been the focal point of my training.

When the start was called, all thoughts other than getting off hard and moving fast went out of my mind. I suppose I somehow reverted to age twenty-one, and when the starting horn went off, I dove accordingly—flat and hard! And of course, my goggles snapped away from my eyes, down over my nose, and popped right into my mouth, severely disrupting my breathing. At that point in the race, there wasn't much I could do about it. To stop and pull them off would disturb the flow of my swimming and could conceivably result in a disqualification. In any event, the time lost would have put me out of the relatively short race. I tried to put my body on automatic and just stay with the flow of things, hoping for the best.

The turn came at fifty meters, and at that point, I was about four or five feet in front, ordinarily a fairly comfortable margin. Even though my air supply had been limited, I was still swimming well. I remember thinking about trying to pull my goggles off at the turn but couldn't figure out how to do it without losing a good deal of time. I opted to keep swimming with my then thoroughly blocked mouth. Bad decision! About four strokes off the wall, the piano * descended. The oxygen debt hit me all at once, and with about forty meters still to go, I was out of air, out of strength, out of everything, and suffering from an extreme case of tightening up.

The pool was only about five feet deep at that end, and I just stopped swimming and stood up. I pulled my goggles out of my mouth and remember placing them rather carefully on my forehead as I watched my competition—all of them—go by. After about seven or eight seconds and the intake of some air, I felt better—no doubt my body's testimony to some basic good conditioning. I remember making a kind of lazy decision to start swimming again. For a while, my stroke came back in gear, and I caught up with the field, perhaps even to the point of being once again in contention, but then quite suddenly, my old friend, the piano, hit with a vengeance. I was about fifteen meters from the finish, and my stroke fell totally apart. The closer to the wall I came, the worse I felt and the more inept I became. I finally finished, but I'm quite sure I was no longer even swimming butterfly. I probably should have been disqualified, but I think the officials were more worried about my health status at that point and actually forgot to critique my stroke for rules violations. Since I was awarded seventh place, I must have even beaten someone. My friend Hal Begal won the race going away.

I was more than a little unhappy with myself. It's a major disappointment when you point for several months toward a big race and then blow it with a bit of stupidity. I did get some satisfaction out of this particular learning experience, however, as I managed to win the one hundred-yard freestyle race four hours later in the day, an event where I really hadn't expected to do much better than third. I learned it was possible to utilize frustration and self-anger and somehow make these emotions the ingredients for top performance. It can work this way in regular life as well, I believe.

It was nice to win the one hundred freestyle, but somehow, it never made up for the race I'd pointed for. But maybe the lessons learned were worth it, who knows? I definitely concentrated more thoroughly on diving mechanics after this meet, and while I'm still never totally free of worry on the point, I've done pretty well getting into the water on starts and keeping those goggles over my eyes where they're supposed to be!

---

*   The piano is swimmer's slang for the painful, temporarily debilitating cramping that occurs during oxygen debt.

Chapter 23

Turns

Unless you're interested in moving into the competitive arena, most of this chapter is superfluous. Generally for lap swimmers, the important stuff is in the first couple of pages of the chapter.

Until you get the skills down pat, turns can be tricky. It's not just a question of swimming to the wall at the other end of the pool and grabbing the gutter, heaving yourself around and pushing off. It can be done that way for sure, but it's bound to be awkward, slow, and part of a swimming pattern that is less than gracefully efficient. There's a right way of changing directions that will make your swimming a lot more enjoyable. There are a number of different types of turns, those more commonly used by lap swimmers and those used in racing. I'll try to cover everything.

Open Turn for Freestyle (Crawl)

This will be the turn of choice for most lap swimmers. It's simple and straightforward. Just swim up to the wall and reach out with your nearest arm and glide or kick right into the wall. Your glide should carry you to the wall without any obvious pulling action of your arm as you reach for the gutter or the wall itself if your pool has no gutter. With your head turned away from your reaching arm, which will bend at the elbow as your upper body moves closer to the wall, let your body take a sideways position in the water, following the lead of your head—left or right. Your reaching arm will now be at water level with your other arm behind and below. At this point, push your head away from the wall, tuck your legs up under your trunk, and place your feet more or less sidewise on the wall about a foot below the surface with your toes pointing in the same direction as your turned head. While your head is above water, take a breath. Let your head and shoulders drop under the surface of the water. At the same time, take your hand off the gutter or wall and bring that arm over the surface and reach out under the water toward the other end of the pool with both arms.

Push off the wall strongly *under* the surface, twisting your body back to horizontal from its sideways inclination as you glide. Reach and stretch out to make your body as streamlined as possible. Pick up your kick as you begin to slow down and start stroking as you break the surface of the water. A good push off should enable you to go at least to the flags, or perhaps even a yard or two beyond, before you break into the air. Don't start kicking too soon. The first part of your glide will be considerably faster than kicking or swimming. You took a breath when your head was out of water at the wall, and now you should let your air out slowly when you begin your kick. Control your exhaling so that you're ready to inhale as soon as you break the surface. (Coaches will recommend that competitors go one-stroke cycle on the surface before inhaling. This sets a good stroke pattern and avoids any gasping or rushed inhaling that would slow the swimmer down. Lap swimmers don't necessarily need to add this bit of torture to their training.)

It's especially important to push off *underwater* where there is less turbulence and where your glide will not be slowed by surface tension. Elegant turns, featuring a long, below-the-surface push off are the mark of an experienced, capable swimmer. An extended, streamlined glide also provides a brief period of recovery from stroking where you can enjoy your aquatic environment, think about feeling the water and ready yourself for the next length of the pool, thinking, "long and relaxed."

Freestyle Flip Turn

The freestyle flip turn is not as hard as it looks, and it has the advantage of actually cutting down on the distance that you need to swim since it's not necessary to touch the wall with your hand, and your momentum will carry you to the wall for a foot touch and push off while your flip is in process. The flip turn is the racer's turn, and it's been proven to be the fastest way of reversing direction in the pool. On the other hand, it's not the turn of choice for most fitness swimmers. One of the problems that must be overcome with the flip turn is loss of air (going hypoxic) as your head is underwater during the turn, and often, there is another lost breath as you sight the wall to gauge your distance prior to making your somersault.

To do the turn, you swim toward the wall; and depending on your height and speed, when you're approximately three or four feet or even farther, from the wall, you'll take your last stroke with one arm, leaving the other arm at your side so that you now are in a head-forward-arms-back position. Do a dolphin kick and duck your head and shoulders. As you duck into the somersault, turn your hands toward the bottom and add an arm thrust to speed the rolling action. The forward arm is the key here. Timed correctly, as you get more experienced with the turn, you'll be able to use your last stroke as one of the main driving forces for the somersault so that the sequence then becomes dolphin kick, duck, and pull—all close together in time.

The key to setting up the flip turn successfully is gauging your distance from the wall correctly as you plan your sequence of moves. Your own height and speed will make a huge difference in determining how far from the wall you should go into your dolphin kick, duck, and pull. Highly trained competitors moving at top sprint speed will start their turns when six feet or more from the wall. (Without goggles, it's nearly impossible for even an experienced swimmer to sight the turn properly. Experienced competitive swimmers understand the critical need for seeing the wall clearly. Neophytes are totally lost unless the turn can be gauged visually with a high degree of acuity.)

As your feet come out of the water, turn your head slightly to one side and coordinate your legs so that your feet find their place on the wall in a more or less upside-down position, toes tilted in the direction you turned your head. Your body position should be in an extended upside-down tuck with your feet on the wall about a foot or so below the surface. You will then reach out with your hands, placing your arms into a streamlined position forward of your head and push off, twisting your body back to its normal freestyle position as you glide. Push off as quickly as possible, and do not try to reposition your feet. *Do your twisting during the glide.* Just as in the open turn, stretch out in the streamlined position, pick up your kick when you begin to slow down, and start your stroking again as you break the surface of the water.

One other tip about the flip turn: when you go into the tuck and bring your legs over, keep them bent. You'll see some swimmers doing the turn with a straight thrusting motion of the legs. They believe they are doing a faster turn this way. Not so. The fastest turn is the one done from a tighter tuck rather than a straight-legged pike position.

It will take some practice, and it's usually best to learn the turning motion out in the pool away from the wall. Once you're familiar with the mechanics, you can begin to do your turns against the wall. At first, you'll find the loss of air uncomfortable during the turn, but the more you practice, the easier it will become. Actually, it's quite surprising how quickly your body will accommodate to the non-breathing period. If you're planning on doing any freestyle racing, this turn is essential. Your competition will be doing it, and it's a lot faster. So it becomes important to do this turn consistently in practice. Otherwise, it will feel awkward when you get to meets.

This is something that most swimmers find that is better learned through the process of imaging. In other words, watching others who do it well. Be aware of the better swimmers where you work out. Often you'll see younger competitors or Masters swimmers doing good flip turns on a consistent basis during their workouts.

Backstroke Open Turn

Like the open turn for freestyle, this is a straightforward, easy way of changing directions, the only problem being the nature of the stroke—looking where you've come from instead of where you're going. In backstroke, you really need those flags, and you need to know where you are from the topography of the ceiling and side of the pool. The faster you're able to go, the more that wall is going to hurt when you crack it with your head! The key is to count your strokes from the flags to the wall. You need to play around with this in practice until you know just where you are in order to develop the confidence needed to do it "blind."

The turn itself is simple. Just glide or kick in with one arm extended, holding the other at your hip. Let your head ride up close to your hand, tuck your feet up on the wall about a foot below the surface, throw your hand and reaching arm back, drop below the surface of the water, and push off into a glide/kick sequence. Since you'll be on your back underwater, you'll need to exhale through your nose to keep it clear. Remember, your glide is faster than swimming. Kick hard for a second or two in order to drive your body to the surface where you'll begin stroking again. And once more, stretch out in a streamlined position to extend your glide.

Backstroke Flip Turn

A few years ago, the rules on turns changed greatly in favor of backstrokers. Prior to the rule change, there were three or four different types of turns being used by backstroke specialists with various arguments about which was faster. There's no argument now. Backstrokers are entitled under the rules to turn over on their stomachs, glide into the wall, do what is essentially a freestyle flip except the feet come directly over the head to land on the wall with toes pointing straight up. This inverted position prepares the swimmer to push off in the correct backstroke position.

The key to making this turn so much faster—thus ending the arguments about the quickest way to do it—is that as in freestyle, no hand touch on the wall is required, and thus the swimmer does not have to swim quite so far. A foot or two less swimming in each length doesn't sound like much, but in a sport where swims are won by inches and hundredths of seconds, this becomes an important factor. Backstrokers are also helped because now they are able to see the wall after turning over on their stomachs, just before the actual turn sequence.

Even more critical than with the open turn is judging your correct distance from the wall for the preparation move where you roll over to your stomach. Here again, use the flags, or lacking flags use a reference point on the ceiling or side of the pool. The rules state that the rollover and turn should be essentially one motion. The inference is that some glide after the rollover is okay, but there is disagreement as to how much kicking, if any, is allowable once you are in a facedown position in the water approaching the wall. This seems to be an issue for the turn judge, and generally, the folks making the judgments are pretty liberal in their interpretations, but disqualifications do occur. The problem rears its head when you misjudge the rollover and find you're still five or six feet away from the wall. Unless you've got an outboard motor tied to your feet, there's no way even an average speedy backstroker will be able to glide that far to the wall. The choice for the swimmer is either to do a little kicking and hope no one is looking or else just lie there dead in the water. The point is—it's really important to know exactly where you are before you start your turn with that rollover!

After you're on your stomach, watch the wall; and at the proper instant, do your little dolphin kick, make your sweeping pull with your outstretched arm, duck your head, and press down with your hands. Be sure there is no twisting motion in your body as your feet come over and out of your tuck. Plant your feet on the wall about a foot below the surface, with your toes pointing directly up. Press your arms forward in a streamlined position close to your head and make a strong push off.

Most of the better backstrokers today use an underwater dolphin kick (on their backs) when their post-turn glide begins to slow. The swimmers who do this well find that they can actually move faster with the kick alone underwater than they can go on the surface doing the stroke. The rules allow fifteen yards (fifteen meters in twenty-five and fifty-meter pools) of this kicking after the start and after each turn. More and more this particular skill is one of the expectations for elite backstrokers. Those who are unable to do it well are at a disadvantage.

I know one young man who is an otherwise very accomplished backstroker to the point of Olympic ambitions. His actual swimming was right up there with the very best, but his underwater dolphin was a weakness. Unfortunately, he never was able to strengthen this skill, a major factor in his not making the 2000 U.S. Olympic team, even though he made the final eight in the Olympic Trials.

After your glide slows, pick up your kick and drive to the surface. Obviously, if you're able to develop a good upside-down dolphin kick, that's the way to go. I wouldn't worry too much about this aspect, however, unless you find you're improving at least to the point that you're becoming a strong local contender in the stroke.

Breaststroke and Butterfly Turns

I'm lumping these two together because they're essentially the same. The important point is that the rules for both strokes require a two-handed touch on the turns—and on the finish. A critical point: any competitor in these strokes should consistently use the two-handed turns—and finish—in practice. We will do in meets what we have done in practice! I've seen many a competitor forget this important point in competition. This is one aspect the judges are unmerciful on. "I just forgot and hit my turn with one hand" is not a happy post-race statement.

It's allowable to lower one shoulder somewhat in anticipation of the turn, but you better touch with both hands simultaneously! After touching, pull the one arm away quickly, bend your knees, and pull your legs in toward the wall and plant your feet sideways. At this point, the turn is very much like the open-freestyle turn. You reach out ahead into a streamlined position in the water and push off while still somewhat on your side in the water, allowing your body to twist back to its normal swimming alignment on the push off.

If you're doing breaststroke, just as you begin to slow in your glide, do a full stroke (all the way back below the hips) underwater with both arms, glide, and bring your hands close to your body returning to the arms out in front position and do a breaststroke kick. Just as you're breaking the surface, begin your arm sequence for breaststroke in the normal manner.

It's permissible under the rules to bring yourself to the surface with this arm stroke, but the rules allow only one arm stroke underwater. It is amazing how far elite breaststrokers manage to travel underwater after starts and push offs. A third of the length of a twenty-five-yard pool is not unusual.

In butterfly, once the glide slows after the push off, the swimmer should start a vigorous dolphin kick. Top competitive swimmers who do this well will utilize the full allowable fifteen yards or meters before breaking to the surface. Swimming even one hundred yards butterfly in a race is extremely taxing. Adding the underwater kicking aspect to it makes it even more so. Most of us find we need to breathe every so often. Most competitors, however, will at least drive to the surface with two to three fairly strong dolphin kicks before picking up their arm action. Generally, recreational swimmers won't be doing much butterfly anyway, much less trying to squeeze the last few yards out of an underwater dolphin kick that is probably more myth than reality.

In General

Good turns add snap and polish to the lap swimmers regimen. You'll feel better in the water when you do them correctly. In all the turns outlined here, strong and long underwater push offs and glides are important. Pushing off the walls is where you should use your legs in swimming. Don't try to get into level, horizontal positions while you're on the wall, but instead, drop well underwater as you push off staying below the drag force of surface tension and turbulence. Except for the backstroke flip turn, push off on your side and twist back into alignment during your glide. Remember, better turns will make you a better swimmer!

Chapter 24

The One-Hour Swim

Triathletes and distance types take notice. January is the designated month for the USMS One-Hour Postal Swim. The One-Hour Swim is a great way to add juice to your distance training. In this chapter, I described my own training secrets that have given me considerable success in this event.

Friends have suggested that I might enjoy a ten-kilometer swim or some really challenging distance like the English Channel or California to Catalina Island. I know better. My aquatic limitations start somewhere around sixty-one minutes of straight swimming and that only after a whole lot of hard work.

Unless you're physiologically strictly a slow-twitch distance type, the training process of convincing your body that you're almost a real distance swimmer can be an interesting challenge. More than anything, it requires a certain brutish determination and willingness to stay with the program, piling on the yardage in the pool and keeping eye to goal for the full ten to twelve weeks it takes.

That's what is needed to prepare for the U.S. Masters National, One-Hour Swim that takes place each January. This is an event that triathletes and accomplished lap swimmers might want to tackle. You can swim it anywhere, even in your own pool as long as the course is at least twenty-five yards long. You need a couple of timers, including someone to attest that you've actually completed a certain distance in the allotted one hour. Your results go in by mail. That's about it.

The thought, however, of undergoing all that pain for the entire sixty minutes can be frightening. My hat is off to some of the folks who are willing to get in there and gut it out after only modest training. There's a lot of torture doing it that way. A better philosophy is to avoid excessive pain in the actual event by subjecting yourself to an element of controlled pain over a more-extended training period.

So you ask, "How can ten weeks of even highly specific training convert you into something that passes for a real distance swimmer?" The ten to twelve weeks mentioned previously assumes that you're not totally out of contact with the water. Many of us even when not in serious training try to swim for fun. For me, this means getting into the ocean or pool three or four times a week and doing 1,200-2,000 yards of fairly relaxed swimming, mixing in some hand-paddle work and kicking. This is a nice comfortable level, and while it won't keep you in competitive condition, it will keep you reasonably fit and provide a base from which to launch serious training over the ten to twelve weeks needed for the distance conversion. If you don't have this base and are starting from scratch, you need to add another four weeks to your program.

Anyone about to start serious distance training should have a basic understanding of distance swimming mechanics: in simple terms, what makes the long-distance swimmer go. Also helpful is some introspective inventory taking of our own personal pluses and minuses. The key, of course, is your arms. This has been emphasized before, but good distance swimmers universally have great pull mechanics. As stated earlier in this book, the kick is less important in distance freestyle; and in fact, too much kicking can be counterproductive. So as you do your self-analysis remember that the arms are key. You will need to learn to use them effectively.

Self-analysis is something we all need to do from time to time. For instance, I know I'm not as strong in the upper body as I'd like to be. My pull mechanics are generally good, and while videos show I set up nicely with a classic high elbow underwater on the left, I'm less than perfect on the right with a hint of dropped elbow. My follow through on both sides is pretty good. So I know what I have to work on.

The dropped elbow, a very common error, means your hand will tend to slip through the water during part of the stroke, leading with the little finger side instead of maximizing water contact. For most of us, the follow through to a point way back on the thigh, below the bottom of the bathing suit, is the first thing to break down in the arm pull when fatigue sets in. The key for me is lots of pulling in workouts. I use big and small paddles as well as some work without paddles. All my pulling is done with a pull buoy, and I sometimes use a lightly inflated inner tube around the ankles to create additional resistance and drag.

A program of lightweights every fourth day can be important. There's no question but dry-land weight work does add strength. Generally, a program emphasizing higher numbers of repetitions and lighter weights will pay dividends in improving endurance. For any swimmer with an upper-body strength problem, Nautilus or weights of some kind are a must. Older athletes need to remember that loss of muscle fiber strength is a fact of aging, but it can be ameliorated significantly with weight training.

When doing a self-analysis, don't forget your breathing! Air is critical! It's safe to assume that most advanced lap swimmers and triathletes already have decent breathing mechanics, emphasizing the exhaling sequence underwater in each breathing cycle, some perhaps even to the point of being practitioners of bilateral breathing. Even so in your self-examination, think realistically about your own breathing mechanics. Do they pass muster?

So what about the legs? For most of us, less is better. Granted, the ideal seems to be a nice deep and rhythmical two-beat kick. Most of us will fall somewhat short here. Try for the two-beat, but even if you find this unnatural, remember to de-emphasize the legs. The place for good kicking is after each turn. Strive for a second or so of forceful six-beat kicking, coming out of each turn as you get back into your stroke. Then back off the kicking and think arms.

During distance events, my own kick is not a driving force for forward momentum, but rather a device for position and balance in the water. I had significant comfort level and time improvement in all races four hundred meters or longer once I learned to de-emphasize my kick, moving it toward the two-beat rhythm. For the one-hour swim, some kick training is needed of course. Remember those push offs! During the ten to twelve weeks training period, the recommendation is to practice your kick about 15 percent of your total workout each day, using a kickboard, doing approximately half your kicking with fins.

One of the things you're going to strive for in your distance training is learning to swim right at your maximum aerobic level (VO2 max). We've covered some of this in previous chapters, but VO2 max is the body's top capacity to maintain exercise strictly from metabolizing oxygen. It was noted that improving this physiological ability to any great degree is unusual. The exceptions might be where someone is significantly overweight or radically unfit physically. Since science tells us that we can expect only a minimal improvement in aerobic capacity no matter how hard we train, learning to swim efficiently becomes even more of a premium.

Maglischo indicates that improvement in anaerobic threshold through proper training is probably the most important conditioning adaptation for better distance performances. The training recommendations made in this chapter do emphasize race-pace training, and too much of this can cause burnout. The question is, what is too much? The answer depends on the individual, but when training for the one-hour swim, I get results from very specific race-pace training every other day done at different intervals to keep it interesting and building up toward some specific goals. Race training for a long aerobic swim is quite different from the demanding anaerobic race training done for shorter events. What the approach outlined here does is to train your body to extend the amount of yardage you can do at the top end of your aerobic capacity (VO2 max).

Step 1: Setting Goals

The first step is setting the right goals. They should be reasonable, yet challenging. Back a few years—when in my fifties and sixties—I had to work pretty hard to get up to around 4,500 yards in one hour. That's an even 1:20 seconds per each one hundred yards, my race-pace goal, the one I trained on for a long time until aging made that pace unreasonable. I would set up with three goals: (1) To swim 4,500 yards in the actual swim; (2) To do a final training set eight to ten days before the swim consisting of forty by one hundred yards on 1:20, holding 1:17 or better; and (3) To do a semifinal set one week earlier than that of eighty by fifty yards on 0:45 seconds, holding 0:40 seconds or better. Written in the "swimmers code," the two sets are the following:

40 x 100 yards at 1:20 swim 1:17 minutes (the final set)

80 x 50 yards at 0:45 swim 0:39 seconds (the semifinal set)

It became clear that when I was able to do the semifinal and final sets with no inordinate stress, the swim itself would not be a problem; the six-day taper and body shave seem to substitute for the short-rest intervals in the training sets.

Setting properly challenging goals can be tricky. If it's any clue at all, my one-hour race pace for 100 yards is about twenty seconds slower than my all-out one hundred-yard time, but I'm not sure how relevant that is for anyone else. You need to think about this aspect and do some testing in the pool. If you have a coach or someone knowledgeable you can talk to, seek advice. A pace goal that is too high will sap your motivation. One that is too low will simply teach you to swim slowly. Perhaps the best approach is to set something a little low at first and be prepared to upgrade your sights and whole program if you're swimming the previously selected paces too easily. There should be some discomfort when you swim a high number of repeats at your VO2 max. This kind of training pushes you into AT territory.

Step 2: Getting into the Program

After setting your goals, the next step is taking the action to follow up on your goals. It's the first of November, and you're just starting out on the program. To be helpful, I'll outline the program I've had success with. A few years ago, my November first might look like this:

> 20 x 50 yards at 0:45 seconds swim 0:40 seconds
> Three hundred yards kicking
> 300 yards kicking with fins
> 20 x 50 yards at 0:45 seconds swim 0:40 seconds (paddles/buoy)
> A total of 2,600 yards

When pulling, I recommend starting with the paddles and dropping them after the first ten fifties, taking a short break between the two sets. A good workout on the next day would involve easy swimming, pulling and kicking, no particular pressure, but with a general goal of building up the total distance to at least three thousand yards. The third day, it's good to move to one hundreds, typically:

> 10 x 100 yards at 1:20 seconds, swimming at 1:17

This is the pace I used when I was in my fifties and early sixties. Realistically today, I've got to settle for slower swimming and allow more time for the set. It's still a question of finding the right goals and sticking to them. Over the training period, your objective should be to decrease the interval at the same time holding to your race pace during the swims in each set. Accordingly, when you begin this kind of training, it might be necessary, for instance, to use a 1:30 second (per hundred) repeat time in training in order to accomplish your goal of swimming at a 1:20 race pace. This might be too fast for some. For others, it might be not challenging enough. The idea is to set a swim and repeat pace that allows for a resting interval of between five and ten seconds.

It takes two or three weeks to get the total distance completed in each day's workout up to the four thousand-yard level. In order for you to condition to swim for an hour, you need to complete total yardage each day that is close to your goal distance. The good news is that with the shorter rest periods between sets and intervals, the time commitment for higher workout yardage is generally less than that needed for sprint and middle-distance training where the emphasis is more toward high-quality swims with longer periods of rest.

Examples: Sets That Work

In about week number four, your conditioning should be coming along and ready for some more serious work. Some of the typical swim and pull sets I recommend are shown below. Remember that these sets are designed for a race pace of 4,500 yards total and based on a pace of 1:20 for each one hundred yards. You should make adjustments for your own ability level.

15 x 200 yards at 3 minutes (alternate swim/pull)

Really concentrate on the pace of 2:40 per two hundred yards during each swim. This is a good bridge set for learning to extend the race pace to longer swims than strictly fifties and one hundreds. I recommend some kicking during your warm up and after the main set during warm down.

10 x 300 yards on 4:30 (swim goal for each interval = 4 minutes)

It's good to alternate between swimming and pulling in each of the ten swims in this set; the pulling should be done with paddles and buoy.

7 x 500 yards on 7:30 (swim goal is again the 1:20 hundred yard pace = 6:40 for each 500)

For this one, it's always swim one/pull one. Don't try to hold the pace on the first or last swim. Use these for warm up and warm down.

   3 x 1,000 yards

Warm up first. The middle one thousand is pulling. Kick two hundred between each one thousand. Warm down. Late in the training period, try to hold a 1:20 pace for each one hundred of the one thousands. In the first few weeks of the program, this will probably be too challenging. If you like swimming long and easy, this workout is suitable for the in-between days. Just swim comfortably; forget the clock.

From this, you should have a pretty fair understanding of the training pattern. Mix in the longer swim sets listed here, but one day each week, try to do at least one set of fifties and one hundreds respectively, building on the number you do each time you train with these sets. Your success in these sets will help you measure your progress. How hard do you have to work to stay on pace and how many repetitions can you do before you fade? These are the two big questions that will give you an index to your progress. Also, you can expect to go through periods when your body reacts badly to the stress. You might feel stiffness in the shoulders and occasionally a spot of dull pain between your scapulae. These are signals to back off for a couple of days.

Handling Stress

All of this presupposes that you're in good physical health and getting regular medical checkups. There's a fair amount of stress in this kind of work. A few years ago when I was training on a 1:20 interval, I began having uncomfortable feelings in my chest, something that made a long-delayed medical checkup the sensible thing to do. Happily, I passed the doctor's stress test with flying colors, but after reflection, I came to the conclusion that it was important for many reasons not to push my body beyond its reasonable capabilities.

Interestingly that year after I quit trying to build my pace to 1:17s on 1:20 in training and dropped back to the 1:19s and 1:20s on 1:25, I did my personal best one-hour swim of 4,555 yards then an age-group (sixty to sixty-four) national record. The inevitable aging process now dictates that I revise my intervals and paces downward even farther as I think through future years' training programs for this event.

One final but important tip. When you do the swim, don't go charging out too fast—a fatal mistake! The piano mentioned earlier in *Good Swimming* can get mighty heavy about thirty minutes into the swim. You've been training on pace. Now's the time to stay with it. In the actual swim, it may be possible to time your start with a pace clock. If you can keep your goggles from fogging, you should then be able to track your progress throughout the hour and particularly in those first few hundreds when you set your rhythm and speed. This can be very helpful.

In conclusion, remember the Masters scene is supposed to be healthy and fun. It isn't fun when you're hurting every day to the point that your body is breaking down and not rebuilding. And logically, we've got to assume it's not healthy. So my final advice for those who may have one-hour inclinations is to give it a try, stick with the training for a while, and if you're making progress and having some fun, go for it.

Chapter 25

Open-Water Swimming for Triathletes and Other Competitors

This chapter is mostly a few tips, aspects of open-water racing that have been helpful to me. Generally speaking, I've found open-water swimming—not just the racing—as among the most pleasurable aspects of this sport.

Open-water swimming is a sport unto itself. It comes in many different shapes and sizes. At its most extreme, there is professional marathon racing where the distances to be covered generally run ten miles or more. Even more taxing are swims such as the English Channel where twenty-one or more miles must be handled, usually in water no warmer than the low sixties. Then there's Lynne Cox, a marathon professional who, a few years ago, did the Bering Straits swim—Little Diomede Island to Big Diomede Island, the United States to Russia, a distance of approximately five miles in thirty-nine-degree water. Without a wet suit!

Then there's the 2.5 mile swim at the beginning of the Iron Man Triathlon. This swim should qualify more in the "fun" category—something doable for most decent Masters swimmers with modest training. The whole Iron Man, of course, gets us back to "extreme."

Open-water swimming can be fun. And it should be, at least for most of us who are not professional marathon racers trying to win prize money. And probably there's a pretty good element of fun for the marathon pros too, considering the prize money in these swims is quite modest, especially when compared to the earnings of professional athletes in many of today's spectator sports. This chapter will focus on less-extreme swims, the kind of events triathletes and Masters swimmers encounter in the warmer months. Most of these really are fun.

The Start

There are a number of ways of starting in open-water races. Sometimes, there's a run to the water. At other times, swimmers crowd behind some sort of rope or ribbon in the water that is dropped or lifted as the gun goes off for the start. I've even been launched from the stern of a rowboat. Then I remember more than fifty years ago the start at the Canadian Exposition professional swim in Toronto harbor. Starting was from a dock into some of the most unappetizing water I've ever seen. The operators of that swim seemingly had little regard for the health of the participants. Even so, unappetizing or not, I did make the attempt, completing about half of the fifteen-mile event before my tank registered on empty.

The start of an open-water swim is usually a confused mass of thrashing bodies with those in the game hoping for a win or at least a high finish aggressively moving to the front. Pity the poor novice who gets caught in this medley of confusion.

The First Part of Your Swim

Whatever method is used to start the race, the first thing you have to decide is how hard to push early. This can be critical. If you take it out too hard at the beginning of a long race, you risk tightening up—going over your anaerobic threshold, resulting in breathlessness and exhaustion—or simply running out of energy and leaving nothing for the finish. What is needed in making the decision is some honest introspection. You must answer for yourself the sometimes-hard question of expectations, are you one of the favorites or more likely to be one of the also rans?

If you've got a shot at winning, it's probably important for you to swim hard right at the gun, particularly if there's a large field. Since the first part of these swims is generally a confusion of thrashing swimmers, the top competitors fight to get out in front where there's smooth water and less chance of being thrown off course by members of the flailing pack. But if the decision is made for a fast start, you need to warm up thoroughly, just as you would for a pool race. A good warm up will protect you against the dreaded tightening up, which, as already pointed out, is a risk that can go with a fast start. Then of course, if you're just one of the many with no real hope of a top finish, it's probably wiser to take your chance in the crowd, beginning the swim at a more conservative pace. A warm-up is still a good idea but not quite so crucial. Some swimmers just use the first few hundred yards of these swims as the warm-up, which means they start slowly and cautiously.

It's tempting to start fast, but it can get you into trouble. A couple of years ago, I made the big mistake of going too hard at the beginning of a swim across Narragansett Bay. I don't know where my brains were at the time, but I decided to start quickly and get to the front of the crowd. The race started with about seventy-five of us standing in chest high water on the Newport side. There was a ribbon marking the starting line, and we all pressed forward waiting for the gun. In my seventies, there was no way I was going to be one of the top finishers, but just the same, for some foolish reason, I wanted to be out in front rather than taking my chances with a lot of body contact in the pack, so I pushed it.

After a couple hundred yards, I realized my error. I was mostly out of the crowd, but I was temporarily exhausted. I wasn't getting my air properly and was in a good bit of pain. I responded by flipping over on my back and swimming backstroke for a couple of minutes. Pretty soon, I recovered and was able to swim proper freestyle again, but as you can imagine, the pack had caught me. I managed to finish somewhere in the middle of the group in this mile and three-quarter swim, but it was a lot more painful than it should have been.

Keeping on Course

One major difference in open-water swimming as compared to the pool is the lack of those nice-lane lines or black guidelines on the bottom to keep you on track. To make the adjustment for proper direction, it's necessary to adopt a slightly different technique. Instead of maintaining your more normal head-down position in the water between breaths, you need to look up and ahead every few strokes, focusing on a landmark in order to keep your direction on track. Of course, if you're involved in a swim where you have a personal guide boat, then it's important to rely totally on the boat, and you should position it on your breathing side and slightly in front. Naturally, you will need a good skull session with your boat crew before the event so they know exactly where you want to swim and how you want the boat positioned. It's a lot easier to maintain proper direction with a guide boat. It's also safer. Then too a guide boat can shield you from the wave action if the day is rough and windy. Having a boat gives you another huge advantage. If you stray off course, you have someone to blame other than yourself.

The rules for some of these swims require that you have a boat and competent crew, usually consisting of a rower and a spotter. Even where it's not required but is optional, try to arrange for a guide boat and crew, assuming, of course, the race is of sufficient length and having a boat is appropriate. Some swims are so short or planned in such a way as to make the boat and crew unnecessary. An example of the latter might be a cable swim where the course is clearly marked with buoys visible from the swimmers' perspective and where the concerns for safety are adequately covered.

But if you're going to do any open-water swimming, you should learn the head-raising technique. This will be a critical skill in open-water swimming where you're not using a guide boat. Learning to raise your head every four- or five-stroke cycles should not be too difficult an adaptation for most. It's something you should try to work on in the pool, lake, or wherever you train. It's important to learn to do this in a relaxed way. It's also critical that you're able to see something when you do raise your head. Since you'll be looking for a building on the shore, a buoy, an anchored boat, or some other landmark, it's necessary to have a good pair of goggles that don't leak or fog up. Many modern goggles have antifog coatings, and there are solutions you can buy which will give the goggles an antifog quality. Even so, I've never found any goggles that remain totally fog free. This can be a particularly difficult problem in cold water. My solution is to swim without them. I've learned to close my eyes when my face is down, and when I come up to breathe or look ahead, I open them, thus sort of blinking my way through an open-water swim. I don't necessarily recommend this style for everyone, however. Most swimmers prefer goggles.

Pace

I've already suggested that you not push too hard at the beginning of a long open-water swim. So what kind of pace works best? Generally speaking, once you get beyond the first three hundred to four hundred yards in one of these races, you should be swimming pretty close to your VO2 maximum, in other words, cranking it along at a speed where you're burning oxygen but not getting into oxygen debt. You should try to stretch it out, stay long with your stroke, make sure you're breathing comfortably, and things aren't hurting too much. You should be swimming at the limit of your comfort zone when you tackle one of these swims.

More specifically, you should emphasize your arms and lay off the legs, particularly if the swim is several miles long. Try to maintain a nice, even pace throughout, and you should have enough left in the last half or quarter mile to pick up the pace a bit. That's when you want to turn on the legs and let yourself swim nearer your anaerobic threshold (AT).

Finding the right pace during the bulk of the event is very important. My guess is that most swimmers who have limited experience in these swims generally are a little too cautious, maintaining a pace and swimming speed that is somewhat slower than optimal, considering their ability.

Drafting

Experienced open-water racers often use a drafting technique. It's thought that as a swimmer moves through the water, because of friction and water tension, a small amount of water will actually move with the swimmer, thus making it possible for a swimmer following closely to receive a boost from the swimmer in front. Drafting is utilized in pool races as well where the competitor to the rear will swim close to the lane line next to the swimmer in the lead. In open-water swimming, drafting seems to have greater application since there are no lane lines, and swimmers can follow directly behind to pick up the greatest amount of boost from the front swimmer. In drafting, it's important to find just the right position. Too far in the rear and you get no benefit. Too close and you're likely to lose some teeth! A kick in the face can be quite painful.

I've never been convinced just how much benefit there is in drafting. I know it can be critical in bicycle racing where racers move at a pretty fast clip, creating what amounts to a head wind that acts to slow the rider significantly. The riders behind get a real benefit from the leader, who is literally breaking out a trail in the air for the riders behind. In the water, where the speeds are slower and medium quite different, there's clearly a benefit, but I've always wondered if the benefit is worth the hassle of maintaining the proper spot behind the lead swimmer. Of more value may be finding the right pace and sticking with it. I'm sure other experienced open-water swimmers might disagree with my viewpoint however, and for sure, you will hear a lot about drafting if you get involved in these swims.

Adjusting Your Stroke

One of the tricks I use when swimming a longer event is changing my stroking emphasis slightly when I feel muscle tiredness, something that usually presents itself as nagging discomfort somewhere in my chest, back, shoulders, or arms. Making a stroke adjustment, emphasizing a part of the body away from the hurting area for a short time, can help relieve the discomfort. This kind of adjustment is subtle, but it seems to work for me. Aches and pains will come and go in these long swims, so you need to be prepared to suffer just a little.

An important factor in stroke adjustment is simply changing the rhythm of your swimming. These changes should be almost insignificant to the observer; however, you, as the swimmer, will both control and feel them. Sometimes, all that is needed is ten or twenty strokes utilizing a slightly different cadence or emphasis to relieve some impending soreness or discomfort, and then you can go back to your more normal way of swimming.

Types of Swims

The variety in open-water swim races is tremendous. In addition to different distances swum, there are course variables. There are cable swims where you go down one side of a line marked with buoys of some sort stretched between two rafts or other markers and then come back the other. The cable might be any distance.

In my Toronto experience of a half-century ago, it was half a mile in length with a raft at each end. I remember there was a terrific melee as swimmers made their way around the rafts. It was pushing, grabbing, tugging, and hauling with little regard for good manners or sportsmanship as competitors tried to get a competitive edge as they made the turn in this fifteen-mile professional swim. The prize money being offered was the obvious motivation for the aggressiveness around those rafts.

There are ocean swims, lake swims, river swims, and bay swims. The nice thing about some of these races is that you actually get the feeling you're going somewhere unlike the sometimes monotonous back and forth of pool swimming. In a river swim, for instance, you get the feelings of swift motion when moving downstream, and you see landmarks pass by quickly. In an ocean, the turbulence of waves presents different challenges and feelings. The variety is part of the charm in this rather strange sport.

Training

One of the aspects I most enjoy in open-water swimming is the training itself. I'm able to get into the ocean in the summer and take long swims parallel to the shore. I tend to swim to certain landmarks on the shore where I have measured out approximate distances and have determined which landmarks to keep my eyes on. Of course, training in the ocean—like the open-water events themselves—is always somewhat uncertain. You have rough days, windy days, cold days, rainy days, and once in a while in the fall, even snowy days. Even after the weather begins to cool down, the ocean tends to remain warm for a considerable time, and I'm generally—even in Rhode Island—able to stay in the water for half an hour or so as late as mid-November. By then the water is cold, and it's wet suit time. If pressed, I'd have to admit that I'm pushing things by swimming in the ocean that late in the year, but I hate to let go of summer. Most of the time, however, even in late fall, it's very pleasant, and some days startling so. Just the same, I'm often glad there's a pool reasonably near for backup.

I really look forward to an early morning swim in the late summer on a warm day when the wind is calm and the sun just up. The water tends to sparkle, and you're able to get into it and just swim. It can be almost a magical experience. When you feel right, you're able to blend with the water, forget everything, and just swim. Those are the "eleven days." They're not all like that, and sometimes, the ocean is so rough and unpleasant that you look at it, then retreat to the pool.

If you're doing most of your training for an open-water swim in a pool, your workouts should follow the same basic regimen I have suggested for the National One-Hour Swim covered in a previous chapter. This means short repeat swims with limited rest periods between each swim in sets as well as days when longer swims are completed. If you're training in the ocean or lake you need to modify this to a degree. You'll probably do as I do: straight distance swims, some kicking, lots of pulling, and a good deal of swimming with fins. Here's where a wristwatch with a visible sweep hand for seconds or, better still, a digital training watch comes in handy. Then you will be able to do some anaerobic work utilizing the watch for your shorter swims. But if you're like me, more of your training will be long swims.

But don't forget the buoy and hand paddles! Distance swims make serious demands on your arms. They need to be in shape, and therefore I recommend that a great deal of your training be done utilizing the hand paddles and buoy. I do at least a third of my ocean training with paddles. There are a lot of different ways of conditioning for one of these swims, but getting your arms ready is a prime tip.

Finishing

How about the finish in your open-water race? Earlier I suggested that you want to save a little gas for the finish. The last quarter mile or so is when you pick up the pace, but don't pick it up too soon. It's okay to go into oxygen debt and tighten up, but *only* as you cross the finish line.

Some of these swims will end at a dock or at a line in the water. The Save-the-Bay Swim in Rhode Island ends in a shallow cove on the Jamestown side of Narragansett Bay. They set up a rather narrow finish area about ten feet wide and mark it with balloons and boats. It's still confusing, and I never have much confidence that I'm finishing in the right place. Going off course near the finish can put you back a whole bunch of places if you're a middle-of-the-pack swimmer as I am these days. This is where you need to be able to lift your head every few strokes, and then you have to figure out exactly where you want to go.

Other swims actually finish on the beach. This is more typical of an ocean swim where you start on the beach and also finish there. In a beach finish where there is a fairly substantial surf running, I've seen folks able to successfully time their finish with a wave and literally ride their way to the shore skipping that sometimes-messy decision about when to stand and run or when to just keep swimming. Riding a wave can also move a competitor up several places in the finish order.

The finish can be crucial, and with beach finishes, you need to save enough energy to get out of the water and make the short run up the beach to the finish line. Don't try to stand up too soon. You're going to be faster swimming until the water gets about knee-deep. At this point, you should be able to move more quickly on your feet as you make your rush to the finish line. On the other hand, one technique used successfully by expert open-water swimmers is to drive toward the finish with dolphin like thrusts. The swimmer, when arriving at waist-deep water, puts both feet on the bottom and thrusts forward, pulling both arms through as in butterfly.

Several such dolphin thrusts should place the swimmer in shallower water where standing and rushing to the finish line is possible.

Warming Down

After the finish of any open-water swim, particularly one where you pushed hard or tightened up during the event, it's a good idea to get back in the water and do some easy swimming. Go slow and stretch it out. A few hundred yards of easy swimming will do wonders in helping you loosen up, thus helping to combat potential soreness in the days to come.

It's always tempting to just ignore the tightness and forget the warm down. I've done this plenty of times myself. The only real downside to forgetting the warm down is you'll feel that open-water swim for a few days afterward, all of which will have a negative effect on your swimming during this recovery period. So if you've got another long swim coming up within a week or ten days of the one you just finished, get back in the water quickly and take a nice leisurely warm down.

Wet Suits

There's one item of equipment that can be important for open-water swimming—the wet suit. The rules for some swims do not allow wet suits; others say fine. Then some swims are done in water so cold it's really essential. In general, if a wet suit is allowed, you should wear one. You'll swim a good deal faster with it than without it. Wet suits increase buoyancy, present a faster surface to the water, and even smooth out some of the body's generally unwanted bulges, thus making for better streamlining. There are all kinds of wet suits on the market. It's a fast-moving technology, but if you're planning on doing some serious open-water swimming, you need one. There are full suits, half suits, suits with arms, suits without arms, thick suits, thin suits, etc. You should decide where and when you're going to swim, be guided by the temperature of the water in which you'll be competing and make a judgment based to some degree on the advice of the sales person. One aspect to keep in mind, however, is that a suit with full arms will limit your shoulder action. In my mind, an arms-free suit is best for racing. Some people disagree, saying that the modern suit allows full freedom for the arms. I'm not convinced and am so dependent on my arms in longer races that I don't want to inhibit them in any way.

Finding Out Where the Swims Are

One question remains: how to discover the whens and wheres of these swims. Here, I'd recommend joining U.S. Masters and your local organization. Clubs have newsletters which detail the wheres and hows of these swims, generally well in advance. There's more information elsewhere in this book on how to join. Go for it. The cost is low, and you'll stay in touch. You'll also meet a fine bunch of people for whom swimming means a great deal.

Open-water swimming is definitely different than pool swimming. For starters, it's much less restrictive, and maybe that's what I like about it, that and the fact that it's a far cry from the sensory deprivation we find in our pools. Open swimming is wide open and full of sensation. Of course, if you're swimming in the ocean, try not to think about sharks and other unpleasant creatures you might confront. I can only say that I've been doing serious swimming in the ocean for well over fifty years, and I've never met a shark. Yet! But I definitely flush any thoughts about these animals out of my mind when I swim. Otherwise, relaxed swimming would be near impossible and not much fun.

Chapter 26

Strength, Flexibility, and Nutrition

This chapter will give the reader some of the basics involving these rather complex subjects. Books have been written about each, but the purpose here is to give the reader at least a surface understanding about the relationship of these matters to swimming.

Earlier in *Good Swimming*, you've read chapters on imaging, relaxing, and developing a feel for the water. These chapters cover some of the more subtle aspects of swimming that while not directly technical are critically important to becoming a better swimmer. Strength is also a vital quality for good swimming. It helps us develop the all-important feel for the water mentioned earlier as well as helping us to become better and faster swimmers. In addition to strength, a certain amount of flexibility also is desirable to help us establish optimal feel for the water and efficiency. Many would add that good nutrition is a requirement for a healthy body able to respond to the stresses imposed by any exercise program. In many ways, strength, flexibility, and nutrition are a three-legged platform that can be regarded as a base for better swimming. We'll deal here with strength first.

Strength

Clearly while you don't have to have the strength of Hercules in order to be a good swimmer, at least normal strength is helpful for the learner. Competition requires something else: greater strength than ordinarily found in the everyday non athlete. Much of this strength needs to be in specialized muscle groups: the long muscles of the back and chest, the shoulders and upper arms and thighs. It's certainly possible for a competitor to become strong enough for competition just through ordinary pool training. Even so, the better competitive swim programs all involve a good deal of weight and other resistance training in or outside of the pool. Strength comes more quickly this way.

I've done it both ways: sometimes with weight training and sometimes without. Further, I have to admit that at this stage in life, I find the discipline required for consistent, specialized strength training beyond my present motivation. There have been periods when I was consistent, putting in solid, two-times-a-week sessions with the weights, and the results were impressive. For a couple of years when I was in my mid fifties, a university coach allowed me to do weight work with his women's team. It was interesting to me to recognize that at that time in my life, I was about as strong overall as most of the women on the team. That meant I could do pretty much the same weight-training circuits the team members did without disrupting the college sessions. The coach had designed a rather complete but simple system involving a progression of workstations. Some of these were free weights, others Nautilus machines, parallel bars, or simply stretching exercises.

I kept at this strength work for about two months prior to the short-course Masters Nationals, and I was delighted with the results I achieved at the meet. My best time drops were in the shorter events, particularly in the fifty-yard butterfly. I suppose this proved a coaching thesis: that strength is particularly necessary for the sprints. Put another way: strength equates to speed. In thinking back over these sessions, I'm sure the strength training regimen was designed by the coach with sprint speed in mind. This makes a lot of sense because so many college races are at fifty and one hundred-yard distances and sprint speed. Strength training is very helpful even at the two hundred-yard distance, meaning that most of the dual meet and conference championship events are covered when sprint-speed strength is emphasized.

The kind of work we were doing was generally lower numbers of repetitions with weights that were fairly substantial in relation to the abilities of each athlete. This training tends to reach and develop muscles that are comprised of fast-twitch fibers. These muscle fibers activate the sprint or speed muscle system. But what kind of work do you need to do to get stronger for the distance events? The basic answer is more repetitions with lighter weights.

But this tends to oversimplify things. In the first place, not all the strength training will be done with free weights or weights in conjunction with a Nautilus or Universal system. Some of this training may be done with resistance supplied through surgical tubing, a swim bench, or swim trolley. To make it just a little more complicated, one of the theories for specific strength training is that on land, it should be designed to mimic the actions of swimming, and that the rate of "turnover" (the rate at which you use your arms) should be the same or slightly quicker than that of the races for which the competitor is training.

It's generally acknowledged that certain types of exercise will give us muscular strength. Muscles get stronger through use. When muscles are exercised, a breakdown of the muscle tissue along with certain chemical activity occurs. Then with rest the muscles rebuild, replacing old muscle fibers with those that are more robust. This is a gross oversimplification of course; but for our needs, it is sufficient to understand that working our muscles hard and allowing for a recovery period has the positive effect of strengthening them.

Another theory holds that adaptations in the nervous system are responsible for much of the strength gains seen in exercise. It is thought that when we use our muscles in hard training, we are somehow opening up neurosystem pathways that enable the body to "recruit" and use more muscle fibers as needed for specific muscular activity. As Maglischo puts it, "As the central nervous system is organized according to movements rather than muscles, it does send messages that call for individual muscles to contract, but the muscles stimulate contractions of certain muscle fibers within these muscles in a sequence that is unique to a particular movement." This is some of the theory behind the concept of specificity in strength training.

The concept outlined in the preceding paragraph is more modern than the weight training I described earlier. I'm sure if that coach was designing his strength training regimen today, it would be more swim-specific-based than it was back then. Even though what I did with the women's team at Brown may have been of a more general weight-training nature than what is recommended today, it was obvious to me that I did indeed receive from that training a significant gain in strength, which I was able to utilize in several meets. I believe the more modern theory results in an improved methodology. Coaches have learned through experience and scientific study how to do it better. A lot of research has gone into finding the most effective methods in strength training for various sports, and in the case of swimming at least, developing exercise regimens for different races.

Assuming what is known today is the most effective pathway for strength gains for swimming, it makes a lot of sense to go with the modern theory.

So how do we mimic the motions of swimming in a strength exercise? Let's start with some strength training ideas that don't take us very far from the pool itself.

Strength Training Done in the Pool

My favorite standby is hand paddles. I've made the hand-paddle recommendation earlier in *Good Swimming* but will reiterate it here. I'm a strong believer in lots of hand-paddle work especially for distance swimmers. Hand-paddle work can make a huge difference for most of us. It's a form of mimicking stroke mechanics where the load factor is light and can, in fact, be varied depending upon the size of the paddles used. A larger paddle results in a greater load and more resistance. Of course, hand paddles (pulling) are a form of pool training. They're definitely not a dry-land regimen. Still, the goal is to become stronger, and paddle work will accomplish that objective. It can be especially effective for the distance swimmer since it obviously mimics the arm action and involves a lot of repetitions at light loads.

The downside aspects of hand paddles are several: they can cause shoulder strains, they can encourage bad mechanics if the swimmer tends to slip his or her hands as they pass through the water without full extension, and it is difficult to maintain a normal turnover rate. Generally speaking, the pluses far outweigh the minuses, and most swim coaches have their swimmers do a lot of paddle work.

Then there are some very basic exercises that can be done right in the water that will make you stronger in ways that will help your swimming. One of the best of these is something I call rise ups. Rise ups start in the water at the side of the pool. After entering the water, face the gutter; next, place your hands, palm down, on the gutter or pool deck about shoulder width and lift your body out of the water. You should make this lift until your arms are fully extended. Hold this extended position for a second or two and then slowly lower yourself back to the starting position. This exercise can be done in sets of any number that seem appropriate to you. For instance, you might start with three sets of ten repetitions. How easy or hard you find this exercise at first will determine both the number of repetitions in each set as well as the number of sets you try at first. In doing this exercise, you should try to let yourself back down slowly after you have raised yourself up. This tends to keep working the muscles over a longer period of time.

Rise ups will develop your shoulders, triceps, and long muscles of the chest and back, all key muscles in good swimming. While this exercise does not closely mimic the stroking mechanics you use when swimming, it will build muscle strength that will help your stroke. In particular, strengthening the muscles needed for the long follow-through, which will contribute to a smooth long stroke. This exercise, like most weight or resistance training, should only be done two or three times a week. If you do it after your normal pool workout, you will build some specific muscle strength without feeling tightness while you're doing your swim workout. If you find this exercise too easy, you could add a weighted belt of some kind.

The drag suit is another device, not unlike hand paddles, used to build strength. A drag suit is a rather heavy suit with pockets designed to catch the water as the swimmer moves forward. This makes swimming more difficult, requiring a greater outlay of muscular effort. A swimmer using a drag suit or other drag device needs to adjust his/her workout to allow for the fatigue that will occur due to the muscular effort being applied. Generally, this will mean repeating shorter swims and taking adequate rest for recovery between each repeat.

The same principle underlies the use of sophisticated machines like the Power Rack. The Power Rack utilizes a belt the swimmer fastens around his waist. The belt is fastened to a pulley arrangement on the machine, which in turn leads to a weight stack. The weight load can be adjusted from light to heavy depending upon the ability of the swimmer. Exercising with this machine, you start with a push off from the wall and sprint for a distance of ten to fifteen yards swimming against the resistance of the weight stack, pulling the stack up its slide to the top. This is fancy stuff, and most of us don't have access to the Power Rack unless we swim in a well-organized team setting.

Less sophisticated, but perhaps just as effective, is swimming against the pull of a long length of surgical tubing. The swimmer wears a belt to which the tubing is fastened. A partner on the deck holds one end of the tubing, and the swimmer dives in or pushes off the wall and swims toward the wall at the other end of the pool. As the surgical tubing stretches, the resistance against the swimmer increases. The last few strokes are, as you can imagine, the most difficult. Generally, the extended tubing will reach the opposite wall of the pool at which point the swimmer turns around and swims back rapidly, enjoying the helping pull of the tubing. It is important, both coming and going in this exercise, to keep your strokes both long and strong. There is a strength benefit in pulling against the tubing and a benefit in the return trip where the swimmer is able to get the feel of swimming at a faster-than-ordinary pace—in other words a feel for speed!

Dry-Land Training (That Mimics Swimming)

Surgical tubing has many uses also in dry land strength training. The most common application is where the swimmer simply pulls against the tubing's resistance. As an example, a swimmer lies facedown on a narrow table or bench, holds on to paddles or handles affixed to the ends of the tubing, the other end of which is fastened to a wall at an appropriate distance. Greater or less resistance can be managed by moving the table or bench further from or nearer to the wall. The swimmer pulls with both arms more or less, mimicking the butterfly stroke. The recovery for each stroke is below the table following in reverse the same arc as described in the pulling phase. The advantage of surgical tubing is that it is fairly easy to maintain a stroke-rate pace, particularly where light resistance is used. If no table or bench is available, the swimmer can stand, bent forward at the waist. The tubing is fastened to a railing, a wall, or some other fixed object. The swimmer then mimics the swimming stroke much as described above.

Another useful device is a swim trolley. This can be made fairly easily. You need to construct a track. I made mine out of a ten-foot piece of two by ten and nailed a four-inch furring piece down the center. Then I constructed the trolley itself out of a three foot two by ten board, screwing two sets of skateboard wheels to the bottom. The wheels ride easily on the track, with the furring piece in the middle centered to keep the "skateboard" contraption from going off into space somewhere. This is important since the machine must be elevated in order to allow room between the track and the floor for the swim stroke. The swimmer lies on the skateboard trolley, grasps the handles or swim paddles fastened with rope or wire to the front of the track. The front of the track is raised higher than the rear to provide the degree of resistance desired. The swimmer then pulls himself and trolley up the inclined plane of the track.

There are many types of swim benches that you can buy. Most of these operate somewhat like the swim trolley described above, having a movable section upon which the swimmer lies. The swimmer, hands in paddles attached to the forward section of the bench, pulls herself forward. The movable section is held back by a length of stretch cord to provide resistance to the exerciser. Adding or subtracting the number of stretch cords can change the resistance level. One highly regarded bench is the Vasa Swim Trainer, which advertises itself as "totally swim specific." Presumably, this bit of advertising histrionics refers to the fact that the machine does indeed mimic the arm action of swimming in its use. The machine comes with a performance meter so that the swimmer can mimic time and pace in training sets. I've seen the Vasa Swim Trainer at pools and at some of the meets where I've competed. It's an impressive device although somewhat high-end in price.

Dry-Land Weight Training (Less Specific)

Free weights and various training machines such as Nautilus, Universal, and Bowflex are some of the equipment that come to mind when I think of weight training. These machines are often quite complex and careful instruction before their use is recommended. Some of these machines are designed to "schedule" resistance at different intensities over the arc of muscular movement. For instance, when using a machine for arm curls, the machine would provide less resistance at the beginning of the curl and a greater amount in the middle of the motion cycle where our arms normally have more strength. The theory is that with some differentiation in the amount of resistance available, the muscles are worked more efficiently leading to greater-strength gains.

I'll say this for the machines. They seem to make the tedious and sometimes painful process of weight training almost fun. But just to emphasize, if you're about to do some work with any of these machines—or for that matter, free weights—for the first time, be sure to get some professional instruction before you start working with them. Ignorance may lead to serious injury. All of the weight centers have exercise pros on staff there to help you. They don't want injured patrons. Coaching is also available at YMCAs and most other places where weight-training apparatus is available.

Free weights have been around for a long time, and they can be useful in strength training for swimming. One of the exercises I like is the bench press, both from the horizontal on-the-back position and from an inclined-plane position. In bench presses, the exerciser lifts the weights from a rack above the exerciser's head. The barbell must be raised off the rack and brought down to the exerciser's chest then raised for the desired number of repetitions. It is most beneficial if both of the motions are done slowly without any bouncing movements. On the press upward, extend all the way. For safety's sake, it's recommended that a "spotter" be in attendance to help in the initial lifting of the weights and depositing them back on the rack. Bench presses develop all-important shoulder strength as well as the long muscles of the back and chest.

There are many different exercises utilizing free weights that can be used to develop strength useful in swimming. For the upper body and triceps, "rows" can be helpful. Here, the exerciser can simply lean forward, usually placing his/her forehead on a brace of some kind to help stabilize the forward-leaning position. The barbell or dumbbells are grasped by each hand so that the backs of the hands are forward. The weights are then lifted to a point underneath the chest.

Crunches, holding a weight on the chest for additional resistance, provide a good abdominal muscle strengthener. This is a simple exercise. Lie on your back on the floor or table with your knees up. Now simply raise your head and chest a foot or so off the floor. You can either hold the raised position for a few seconds or drop your chest back to the floor and repeat. Again, this exercise should be done in sets—perhaps ten crunches in a set for five sets. Crunches will exercise the upper abdominal muscles. Leg raises will do the same for the lower abs. For leg raises, simply, while lying on your back, curl your knees up to your chest, then straighten your legs, bringing them to a point two or three inches off the floor or table. Hold that position for a few seconds, and then let your legs fall to the floor or table. Repeat. Again, leg raises should be done in sets. Weights can be added at the ankles.

Half-knee bends while holding on to a barbell or dumbbells will strengthen your legs, particularly the muscles on the front of your thighs. These are the muscles used in push offs on turns and starts as well as for power in kicking. Toe raises will work the muscles of the lower leg and add power to your starts and push offs. The toe raise is a simple exercise. You stand on the floor and rise up on your toes. Holding dumbbells or a barbell will add resistance.

These are just a sampling of some of the more important exercises that can be done with free weights. As I stated earlier, it is thought to be more effective to do weight work that more closely mimics the action of swimming. Thus, land work with surgical tubing or the swim trolley is highly recommended. And once more, remember my strong recommendation for the use of paddles and a buoy in the water. These exercises will make you stronger and accordingly a better swimmer.

Stretching

This is a personal preference subject. Some athletes are stretch fanatics. I'm not. I'm impressed that Maglischo even waffles on stretching: "Although joint flexibility is believed to be important to efficient swimming, there is, once again, little scientific evidence to substantiate that belief." Maglischo goes on to offer some rationale for stretching as an assumed benefit for better swim performance, citing improved range of motion in the joints as allowing for more propulsive stroke mechanics, "fewer disruptions in horizontal and lateral alignment" thus reducing drag and better energy pay off because internal resistance to motion is reduced.

One important cautionary note about stretching: when doing a stretching exercise, don't push in little bouncing spurts in an attempt to extend the stretch itself. This can cause muscle tears or even damage to the tendons or other connective tissue in your joints. The proper way of stretching is to hold the arm or leg in a manner that challenges the joint's normal range of motion. A partner can often be utilized to help. The idea is to hold the limb in this position slowly pressing *almost* to the point of pain. After about thirty seconds or so, you should feel the tension in the arm or leg disappear. There's a definitive feeling of relief that comes about in most of these stretching exercises as the tension is released. Perhaps that's why they're so popular with some folks. But again, stay away from the bouncing action.

In any case, most of the stretching exercises are simple. I do several, mainly because my hamstrings are a lot tighter than ideal. Stretching to touch your toes is the answer to the hamstring problem. You stand with your legs straight and bend at the waist reaching as far down as possible in an effort to touch your toes. I can usually touch my ankles and have always envied those who can place their hands flat on the floor rather than merely touching their toes. The exercise can also be done sitting on the floor and reaching forward to your toes.

Shoulder flexibility can be improved utilizing an exercise that includes a towel. Hold the towel in front with your hands fairly wide. Raise your arms and continue over your head and behind your back. This may be difficult at first, and you may have to separate your hands farther in order to complete the exercise. The idea is to be able to decrease the space between your hands over a period of time.

I have spoken in earlier chapters of *Good Swimming* (see chapter 23, "Turns") about "streamlining" and maintaining a streamlined position in the water. Here is a simple exercise that will help. Standing on the floor, raise up on your toes and extend your arms toward the ceiling. Place one hand over the other. Your upper arms should press against your ears. Really reach up and stretch. Your legs should be together. If you have trouble holding the stretched position and maintaining your balance, the exercise can be done with a wall at your back. Try to hold the position for ten or more seconds. Repeat the stretch several times.

Here's another shoulder exercise many swimmers use to stretch the shoulder joint, the triceps, and the long muscles of the chest and back. Put one hand behind your neck and grasp your upraised elbow with your other hand. Apply pressure by pulling your elbow toward your head, hold the position; and when you feel the tension release, apply a little more pressure.

There are a number of exercises designed to increase ankle flexibility and range of motion. The simplest of these involves standing several inches in front of a wall with your feet pointing toward the wall. Lean forward without raising your heels. Hold on to the wall so that you will not fall. You will feel pressure in the calf muscles and Achilles tendon. Be careful; don't overdo it. Things can pop.

Another exercise for the ankles involves getting into a kneeling position with your ankles under your gluteus (butt). Lean backward. You will feel pressure in the flexor muscles and along the front side of your shins as your ankles stretch out as though pointing.

And still, another effective stretching exercise to increase ankle flexibility is something I call toe pointing. From a seated position, raise your leg and point your toes. Now make circular motions with your foot as though you were trying to draw small circles with your big toe. This stretch can be done either one leg at a time or with both legs together.

These are just a sampling of the stretching exercises that can be done. If stretching is your thing, I'm sure imagination and ingenuity will enable you to come up with dozens of ways to stretch out your joints and muscles. Stretching is, I believe, another way of making that all-important somewhat hackneyed statement we've heard that goes along with aging and exercise mechanics generally, "If you don't use it, you'll lose it!" Certainly, stretching is part of using it. I should probably do more of it.

Nutrition

This is a big subject. Many books have been written on it. Generally speaking, the diet for any athlete should contain enough of the basic nutrients to handle the energy output required for training and competition. This means proteins, carbohydrates, fats, vitamins, and minerals and, of course, sufficient fluids. The big question is deciding on how much of each is optimal. The answer depends to some degree on our own individual bodies. Are we overweight, underweight, or just about normal? How hard are we going to be working on our swimming?

These are just some of the questions each of us must answer in determining our individual dietary needs. And it can get pretty confusing when you start looking for some guidance on the subject. You can easily find books hyping all kinds of diets—diets that emphasize proteins, diets that push carbohydrates, normal diets, vegetarian diets, cancer-controlling diets, heart-health diets, etc. Unless you're a person with some kind of special nutritional need, the normal diet for an athlete probably should run two-thirds or more to caloric intake from carbohydrates with the remaining third consisting of more protein than fat.

It's easy to go overboard on the subject of diet, but generally speaking, if you eat a normal balanced diet that has some emphasis on fruits and vegetables, you'll do just fine. This assumes you'll be eating your regular quota of meats for protein. It's all too easy to sneak too much fat into our diets of course, so sometimes, it's necessary to emphasize one aspect and cut back on another. It helps to know something about the categories of the food you're eating.

Proteins include meats, cheese, eggs, fish, poultry, milk, beans, peas, nuts, and cornmeal. Carbohydrates include fruits, vegetables, bread, honey, potatoes, rice, spaghetti, and sugars. Fats include oils, sweets, fat in meat, cream, gravy, and many "munchie snacks." This is an abbreviated list, and you will note there is overlap among the categories with some foods supplying the needs in two categories. Also, it is generally recommended that we try as much as possible to fill our carbohydrate needs from vegetable and fruit sources, including the starches, rather than from the sugar forms. As Maglischo puts it, "With starch as your primary energy source, a higher work rate can be maintained for a longer period, symptoms of hunger are reduced, and replacement of liver and muscle glycogen proceeds at a faster rate." Starches are plentiful in bread, corn, wheat, rice, potatoes, and other root vegetables.

These are some general dietary tips. Unless the level of your training is going to be on the high end of intense, there's really no need to do much more than take a good introspective look at how you're eating now, making any minor or major changes you feel are appropriate to good health and weight control. I mention weight control because a great deal of attention in the media has pinpointed obesity as a major problem in the United States. It also gets a lot of attention from many coaches as they prepare teams for competition. Daily and/or weekly weight checks are often mandatory. Coaches do not like to see their swimmers becoming overweight. An overweight swimmer is a slower swimmer. Extra weight also makes us more injury prone.

Weight can become a problem in high-exercise settings. The demands of intensive training are often felt at the dinner table with eating getting out of control. This is something we all need to watch when we're involved in an exercise program. There is another more insidious problem that occurs when we stop or back off from intense periods of training. We get used to eating more, yet in reality, our bodies no longer need the high caloric intake that has become our habit. The result can be a rapid weight gain. This is something I try to watch closely since like most of us, my own training varies from moderately intense to low-key maintenance throughout any given year.

Fluid intake is critically important when we exercise. The more intensely we train, the more fluid we will lose, mostly through perspiration (and yes, we do sweat when we work out in the water), our breath, and kidneys. Having this in mind, it's a must to replace the fluid loss. Water is the number one recommendation here although there are a number of "energy drinks" on the market that will replace certain minerals we also lose while exercising. Many athletes swear by them. Water, however, is the basic need to keep us properly hydrated. We should remember that our bodies often need water even when we do not feel thirst.

Many swimmers like to bring a water bottle to the pool so that they can take sips from time to time. This works fine. If you don't follow this practice, remember to hit the fluids hard whether you feel thirsty or not when you get through working out. The need for fluid does not always quickly manifest itself with thirst.

One other nutrition subject to think about is vitamins and other supplements. Many doctors will tell you that if you are getting well-rounded meals with lots of fresh fruits and vegetables, you don't really need to worry about supplements. I'm not so sure. I have added a multivitamin and something called Juice Plus to my daily regimen of things I take. I feel pretty good taking these things, and I'm more than a little afraid to stop. Like most old timers, I suffer from some osteoarthritis, particularly in the hands. Glucosamine/chondroitin (triple strength) seems to help. I gulp when I see the cost, but the pain in my hands is a lot less. Maybe we older folks just need more of this supplementation.

I've also become a huge believer in vitamin D (actually D3 or cholecalciferol). I got started on that after meeting a vitamin D researcher from Canada on a trip. It seems he was getting good results using fairly large doses of this vitamin (2,000 IU per day) with men like me who have prostate cancer. Right now, I'm taking a lot more than this dose and my formerly rising PSA seems to have gone on hold. I'd suggest that any man with prostate cancer might do well to talk to his doctor about vitamin D. My internist thinks I'm crazy taking these big doses, but I'm getting encouragement from two oncologists and am getting regular urine and blood tests to check on the safety and effectiveness of what I'm taking. There's a lot of testing and new information coming out on vitamin D, and most of the professionals in the know say that those of us who live in the temperate zones are not getting anywhere near enough of this sunshine vitamin.

While different physicians may have different takes on the use and need for supplements, probably the best guidance you can get is your own family doctor. He or she will know you best and therefore will know your individual needs best.

In Summary

All of this really just brushes the surface of these important and interesting topics. Perhaps what you've read here will lead you to further research and investigation. Strength gains coupled with heightened flexibility along with proper nutrition can be the mainstays to better swimming, not to mention better health and a happier life. For most of us, I suspect the better health and happier life is what we're really looking for in our sport of swimming. That most of us want to do it better is mainly a question of self-satisfaction, a pride in doing well. But in addition, the biofeedback we get from doing it well or to put it more simply—feeling good in the water—adds a tremendous joy to what otherwise might be "just exercise."

Chapter 27

Goals and Other Conclusions

There are some applications here that work in real life too.

This could have easily been the first chapter as well as the last, but then this whole book has been full of talk about goals and goal setting. The concept of setting objectives and working for them is a formula for success in all walks of life. It's not just the recipe for better swimming although it certainly is all of that. Certainly, the value of setting goals was one of the lessons I learned early on as a competitive swimmer.

My son, who was a decent swimmer in high school, probably didn't learn the lesson until recently. Now just fifty, he's a pretty good salesman. When we sit down and talk about his work, he's full of chatter about this goal and that objective. It didn't used to be so. But since he's begun thinking this way, he's been selling up a storm, and his paycheck is showing it!

From my locker-room discussions, I get the feeling that most fitness swimmers don't think much about their goals—at least insofar as they apply them to their swimming. I get the impression that for many, it's just some vague idea that getting into the pool every day, two or three times a week or whenever, will somehow add something to their lives. And it probably does, but I often wonder if these folks ever think about what they really want to accomplish with all that swimming.

So that's my first suggestion: think through what you want from your swimming. Perhaps you're only looking for a few moments of peace and quiet, a place where you can put out a little energy and let the water flow around your body as you move gently through it. And that's not an unworthy objective, but my point is to suggest that you should examine what you're doing and why you're doing it. The mental exercise will tend to keep you focused and more in tune to your goal, what ever it may be.

Let's face it, going to the pool, getting undressed and into your suit, taking a shower, doing your workout, taking another shower, getting dressed again, and then driving home or to the office takes something of a major effort. It's three hours, counting driving time, out of my day. That's one-eighth of every twenty-four-hour period on a near daily basis! With that kind of a commitment, I better darn well understand what I want out of it, have some pretty clear goals in mind, be focused on them, and have an expectation of some success in meeting them.

Overall, I've been at the reconstituted competitive swim game for some thirty years, and my goals today are different from what they were when I first started. In fact, they've been recast a number of times along the way. I started out looking for a conditioner with just a salting of competition for flavor. I went through a period when competition meant a great deal, and I worked very hard at it and was willing to put up with a good deal of pain in workouts in order to meet the success I was after in races. But now my approach is more mellow.

For instance, when I planned and set my goals for a United States Masters Short Course Championships a few years ago, I did an introspective reality check. I knew that there were at least two other middle distance swimmers who would be more than I could handle unless I was willing to make an extreme training commitment. I'm at a point in life where double workouts and yardages much over three thousand per day hold little appeal. I felt that by focusing my quality sets on my butterfly specialty but avoiding injury by not overdoing it and adding some endurance training, I would be able to place reasonably high in the longer freestyle races and would have a good shot at winning my one hundred-yard butterfly event. I set my daily training objectives within the parameters of these overall goals, and it worked out fine. I won my butterfly and took seconds and thirds in the longer freestyle events. And most important, the meet was fun.

One of my subsidiary and longer goals was the need to improve my butterfly kick. My vision of modern-day butterflyers and backstrokers cranking out their underwater dolphin kicks juxtaposed against the memories of some problems I'd had kicking into walls during races, underscored for me that it was time to do some serious kicking. So I set a goal and had some fun with it too!

After each workout, I started doing one length of underwater dolphin kicking. Of course, the first time I tried it I only went about fifteen meters.

Early improvement was slow and grudging, but after a month or so of this, I finally made the full twenty-five-meter distance—a major success. After making the distance about five days in a row, I reset the goal. It was time to put the clock on it. Using the pace clock, I discovered it took me forty seconds to kick the twenty-five meters underwater. That became my baseline. Over the next month, my time for the "event" gradually came down. Just before I left for the nationals, nicely rested, I was able to do it in twenty-eight seconds. Not a great time for a young collegian, but for a geriatric butterflyer, not bad! In the one hundred-butterfly at the short-course championships, my "new" kick helped me win the event comfortably. As was often the case for me in this race, I was a little "short" on two of my three turns and the finish, but I felt good acceleration when I applied the kicking power to drive me into the wall each time.

We need to be careful when we set goals. They should be challenging but not out of reach. Unreasonable goals do not motivate us. And presumably, motivation is one of the reasons we set them in the first place.

So what do you want out of your swimming? Is it a question of peace and quiet? Are you looking for health, fitness, and feelings of well-being? Do you want to become stronger? Do you want to improve to the point that perhaps you could become a competitor on the Masters circuit? These are the overall goal/objective questions only you can answer for yourself. Once you've established your basic objectives, then you can chart the route for meeting them.

And right now, I'm strictly a lap swimmer. As I write, summer is here, and it is downtime for me as a competitor. My goals for the summer include enough swimming to keep a sense of fitness and to stay in contact with my sport so that when I want to crank it up again in the autumn, things will fall back in place fairly easily. I'd also like to get my golf game down into the low eighties with regularity, but that would definitely be categorized as an unreasonable goal. My swimming goals, however, are quite reasonable.

Meeting my fitness swimmer objectives outlined above is really quite simple. I will get into the ocean or pool at least four times a week and will do varied workouts, mostly distance oriented, with some kicking and pulling with paddles, very little sprinting, and only a modest amount of butterfly, and that with fins in order to avoid injury. That's all there is to it, but I have to make sure it happens. Basically, that's not a problem because swimming is an activity I enjoy. The clear delineation of this rather easy goal means I can get away with a minimal amount of planning for each workout.

Some people like to plan their workouts very carefully. I see men and women coming into the pool with daily workouts written out on paper. It's probably the right approach for most of us. I might do better that way myself, but since I usually can remember what I did the day before and will want to do something different today, I like to fly by the seat of my pants. I usually plan out my workout—my goal for the day—driving to the pool, often putting the finishing touches on the plan while I'm in the shower, and sometimes, those warm showers can tempt me into long-planning sessions.

I'm not suggesting that everyone should do it my way, but I am suggesting that planning—daily goal setting—is important. As you set your goals each day, try to remember what you did the two or three days before and plan something different this time. Doing the same thing every day encourages boredom and does not train your muscles as effectively as varied workouts.

I hope I've convinced you to do a little more goal setting. I think you'll enjoy the challenge of doing things on an objective/result basis. There really is great personal satisfaction when you've accomplished an objective that when originally set seemed challenging. I know I got a lot of satisfaction out of my peculiar little goal for underwater kicking. It was a daily challenge and almost daily satisfaction, all of which made it fun.

We should enjoy our swimming. It should be fun. I think you'll enjoy your own swimming more if you're able to do it more skillfully. I hope this book helps. I enjoyed writing it.

Appendix

A Workout Sampler

Richard Burrows, now a lawyer and always a swimmer of considerable prowess, was a swim coach in an earlier professional life: first with Little Rhody Swim Club and then at Denison University. In this latter position he earned the prestigious NCAA Division III "Coach of the Year" award in 1986. In his three years at Denison he coached two Division III National Champions and 20 of his swimmers made Division III All-America.

Rich has been coaching John Forasté, the photographer for *Good Swimming*, for several years. John has kept a complete library of the workouts designed by Rich. I'm indebted to them both: to Rich for allowing them to be used in my book and to John for suggesting that they might be helpful. I present them here as I received them in no particular order, written in coach's code — or shorthand — with little notes to me that help in the explanation. I have occasionally added my own comments. These workouts were done in a 25 meter pool; for yards the time intervals should be adjusted down about 10%.

Coach Burrows designs these workouts and sets the intervals for himself, then emails them to John who swims the sets, but modifies some of the times as needed. John is a workout swimmer in his early 60s and in good shape, but no longer competes in Masters. His genetic-muscle cell makeup would seem to place him more in the slow-twitch or distance swimmer category. This having been said, you will find information about how to adjust the intervals in Rich's workouts to your own unique abilities in Chapter 20, "Training: The Clock Is Your Friend" and Chapter 24, "The One Hour Swim."

Good luck and enjoy!

Win, ETOF means Every Third One Fast.

1. Warm-up	150 swim, 150 pull (no paddles), 150 drill, 150 kick
2. Swim	4 x 100 on 1:40 descending
3. Pull with small paddles	4 x 150 on 2:30 descending
4. Kick	12 x 25 ETOF on 0:35
5. Swim	4 x 100 on 1:50 descending faster than # 2
6. Kick	12 x 25 ETOF on 0:35
7. Swim	4 x 100 on 2:00 descending faster than # 5

(3,000)

Win, as you know, negative split means the second half is faster than the first.

1. Warm-up	500 (middle 200 drill)	
2. Challenge Set		
	Swim	4 x 125 on 2:00
	Kick	1 x 100 on 2:00
	Drill	1 x 50 on 0:60
	Swim	4 x 100 on 1:30
	Kick	1 x 100 on 2:00
	Drill	1 x 50 on 0:60
	Swim	4 x 75 on 1:10
	Kick	1 x 100 on 2:00
	Drill	1 x 50 on 0:60
	Swim	4 x 50 on 0:45
	Kick	1 x 100 on 2:00
	Drill	1 x 50 on 0:60
3. Pull	1 x 400 negative split by 5 seconds or more	
4. Swim	4 x 25 on 0:45 sprint!	

(3,000)

Win, you'll notice that he sends sweet little comments from time to time too.

1. Warm-up   12 x 50 on 0:60 – 4 swim, 4 pull, 4 drill

2. Swim   4 x 100 on 2:00 descending

3. Pull   2 x 400 on 6:30 negative split by 10 seconds

4. Kick   1 x 800 free under 15:30

5. Swim   4 x 100 on 2:00 faster than in # 2

(3,000)

John, are you in shape yet? Can you still make 100s on 1:30?

Win, EFOS means Every Fourth One Sprint. A shorter than usual workout compensates for it being a "quality workout" with some speed work.

1. Warm-up	200 swim, 200 pull, 200 drill, 200 kick
2. Swim	10 x 50 alt. slow on 1:30/FAST on 0:60
3. Pull	4 x 150 on 2:30

1st – with big paddles, tube, buoy

2nd – with small paddles, tube, buoy

3rd – tube, buoy

4th – buoy

4. Kick	16 x 25 on 0:35 EFOS!
5. Swim	10 x 50 alt. slow on 1:30/FAST on 0:60

(2,800)

Win, while IYATE means If You Are Tough Enough. IYAAW means If You Are a Wimp. Cute. And, as you know, descend means that each swim in the set is faster than the one before.

1. Warm-up   10 x 50 choice on 0:60

2. Pull   4 x 500 negative split and descend on 7:30 (or 8:00 IYAAW).

3. Kick   8 x 50 on 0:60

4. Swim   4 x 25 FAST on 0:45

*Fin day will be Tuesday this week since my fins are in my car, and my car is in the shop until Monday.

(3,000)

Win, notice the way he plays around with the math. This day was based on 400s. N.S. means negative split.

1. Warm-up	8 x 50 on 0:60
2. Pull	1 x 400 on 6:00 – N.S.
	4 x 100 on 1:30
	8 x 50 on 0:45
3. Kick with fins	1 x 400 back on 6:00
	16 x 50 – 4 on 0:50, 0:40, 0:45, 0:40
4. Swim	8 x 50 – 2 on 0:45, 0:50, 0:45. 0:60

(3,200)

Win, in the pull set, notice that the distance decreases as the difficulty increases.

1. Warm-up   10 x 50 alt. drill on 0:60/swim on 0:50

2. Pull   1 x 400 with big paddles, tube, buoy on 6:30

                      1 x 300 with small paddles, tube, buoy on 5:00

                      1 x 200 with tube, buoy on 3:30

                      1 x 100 with tube only under 1:40

3. Kick with fins   3 x (4 x 50* on :45, 1 x 200 free on 3:00)

                      * 1 set back, fly, fly on back

4. Swim   2 x (2 x 50 breast pull with fly kick on 0:60,

                      1 x 150 on 2:15)

(3,200)

Win, another signature of Rich's workouts is that Monday is fin day. And he usually increases the total distance to offset the less difficult fin set.

1. Warm-up   8 x 50 on 0:50

2. Pull with big paddles   1 x 1500 – hold under 1:30 per 100

3. Kick with fins   4 x 250 on 3:45 – alt. back, free, fly, free

4. Swim   8 x 50 on 0:50 faster than # 1

(3,300)

Win, alternating slow/fast and fast/slow (in the 5th set) really works. You feel ready for the fast after the slow, but then need the slow to recover and get ready for the next fast one.

1. Warm-up   12 x 50 on 0:60 alternate swim, drill, kick

2. Swim   1 x 500 negative split under 7:30

3. Pull with small paddles   2 x (2 x 25 breast on 0:45, 1 x 300 negative

                        split on 4:00)

4. Kick   8 x 100 free on 2:00

5. Swim   8 x 50 on 0:50 alt. slow/fast, fast/slow

(3,000)

Win, EFOS means Every Fourth One Sprint.

1. Warm - up	1 x 800
2. Pull with small paddles	1 x 400, 300, 200, 100 – on 6:15, 4:45, 3:15, under 1:30
3. Kick	1 x 400 free EFOS
4. Swim	16 x 50 – 4 on 0:45, 0:55, 0:45, 0:60

(3,000)

Win this is an excellent pull set, one he sticks in from time to time. And, again, alternating easy/all out is very effective. Here also is his signature pull set that ends with the tube only (which is not easy). This is an overall great set.

1. Warm-up   12 x 50 on 0:60 – alternate swim, drill, kick

2. Swim   4 x 100 on 2:00 alt. easy/ALL OUT and FAST for time!

3. Pull   4 x 200 on 3:30

              1st – big paddles, tube, buoy

              2nd – small paddles, tube, buoy

              3rd – no paddles, tube, buoy

              4th – tube only

4. Swim   8 x 50 on 0:60 alt. easy/ ALL OUT and FAST for time!

5. Kick   1 x 400 IM under 7:45

6. Swim   16 x 25 on 0:30 alt. easy/ ALL OUT and FAST for time!

(3,000)

Win, I find it interesting that, while the workouts are usually 3,000, the amount of ink it takes to write the workout can vary greatly.

1. Warm-up	400 choice
2. Pull with big paddles	4 x 300 on 4:30
3. Kick	4 x 150 on 3:00 – 1 each stroke
4. Swim	2 x (6 x 50 on 0:50, 1 x 100 on 1:30)

(3,000)

Win, swimming freestyle while crossing your feet is not easy.

1. Warm-up	100 swim
	2 x 50 drill
	100 swim
	2 x 50 cross feet
	100 swim
	2 x 50 kick
	(10 seconds rest between each)
2. Pull with small paddles	5 x 200 on 3:10 negative split and descend
3. Kick	1 x 800 IM
4. Swim	5 x 100 on 2:00 alt. IM/free/IM/free/IM

(2,900)

Win, lots of descending times. EFOS means Every Fourth One Sprint.

1. Warm-up	300 swim, 300 pull, 300 kick
2. Swim	3 x 100 on 1:40
	3 x 100 on 1:35
	3 x 100 on 1:30
3. Pull	4 x 150 descend on 2:30, 2:25, 2:20, under 2:15
4. Kick	16 x 25 – 4 each stroke on 0:35 EFOS
5. Swim	8 x 25 – 2 each stroke on 0:30

(3,000)

John, Are you back into the swim of things?

Win, lots of ink, but still the usual 3,000. I never asked Rich to actually define Success Drill.

1. Warm-up		150 swim on 2:30, 3 x 50 pull on 0:50
		150 swim on 2:30, 3 x 50 kick on 1:10
2. Success Drill	Swim	4 x 100 on 1:40 – descend
	Easy	2 x 25 on 0:30
	Kick	2 x 50 free on 1:15
	Swim	4 x 100 on 1:35 – descend
	Easy	2 x 25 on 0:30
	Kick	2 x 50 free on 1:15
	Swim	4 x 100 on 1:30 – descend
	Easy	2 x 25 on 0:30
	Kick	2 x 50 free on 1:15
3. Pull		1 x 200 on 3:30 – small paddles, tube, buoy
		2 x 100 on 1:45 – small paddles, tube
		4 x 50 on 0:50 – tube only
4. Swim		6 x 25 on 0:45 alt. count/fast-2 breaths max

(3,000)

Win, warm-up, swim, pull, kick, warm-down. A recognizable pattern.

1. Warm-up	150 swim, 150 pull-no paddles, 150 drill, 150 kick
2. Swim	2 x 200 * on 3:30
	2 x 150 * on 2:30
	2 x 100 * on 1:30

3. Pull with small paddles

          3 x (1 x 100 on 1:40, 2 x 50 on 0:50, 4 x 25 on 0:25)

4. Kick/Swim	2 x (2 x 50 kick on 0:60, 4 x 50 on 0:45)
5. Warm-down	4 x 25

* 2nd faster than 1st

(3,100)

Win, Set 3 with tube only, tube and buoy, tube and buoy and paddles, is a little signature of Rich's, though he usually does it in reverse order, ending with tube only (the hardest).

1. Warm-up	150 swim, 150 pull (no paddles), 150 drill, 150 kick
2. Swim	4 x 150 on 2:30
3. Pull	3 x 300 on 5:00
	1st – tube only
	2nd – tube, buoy
	3rd – tube, buoy, small paddles
4. Kick	12 x 50 on 0:60 – 3 each stroke
5. Swim	4 x 75 on 1:25

(3,000)

Win, r.i. means rest in between.

1. Warm-up	2 x (100 swim, 50 drill, 50 cross feet, 50 kick) – 10 seconds r.i.
2. Success Drill	Swim 6 x 50 on 0:55
	Drill 1 x 100 on 2:00
	Kick 1 x 100 on 2:00
	Swim 6 x 50 on 0:50
	Drill 1 x 100 on 2:00
	Kick 1 x 100 on 2:00
	Swim 6 x 50 on 0:45
	Drill 1 x 100 on 2:00
	Kick 1 x 100 on 2:00
3. Pull with small paddles	3 x 200 N.S. and descend on 3:15
4. Kick	1 x 200 free ALL OUT under 3:35
5. Warm-down	4 x 50 on 0:60 ascending

(3,000)

POSTSCRIPT FOR CHAPTER 25
OPEN WATER SWIMMING

John Forasté, photographer for this book and something of an open water maven, noted that in Chapter 25, Open Water Swimming, I had not said much about how to deal with the more than occasional rough water you will incur in open water events. It was probably some kind of Freudian slip on my part. I end up swimming in rough water a lot and I don't care for it, especially when you're faced with a windy slop coming at you from your breathing side.

This brings up my first piece of reasonable advice: learn to breathe on both sides. Of course this has been discussed in other chapters as a highly recommended way of learning to swim more smoothly, but you are pretty defenseless in an open water swim if you're swimming into rough slop pounding into your face when you try to breathe.

The other technical thought that's especially important in rough water swimming is to maintain good high-elbow technique. The high elbows will not only enable you to swim better, but you will be able to make a smoother recovery on each stroke as your arms are more able to clear the inevitable wave action of water.

John's way of dealing with the rough water in his swims is to "go with the flow." I think by this he means to not fight the water, but to maintain a long, steady stroke and relaxed breathing. This makes good sense. Then of course, if it gets treacherously rough maybe it's time to think about putting an end to your swim, although usually the people running the event will take care of that for you. From my very personal perspective, a long swim in rough water is not fun and it can be dangerous.

INDEX

WIN WILSON SWIM RESUME

US Masters Swimming

In his thirty years of competition, starting in 1975, Wilson has won over 150 national and world championships in freestyle, butterfly, individual medley events, and team relays. He set approximately twenty-five national and world records in various individual and team-relay events. He has been awarded the Masters All-American designation every year in his thirty years of competition. In 1983 and 1984, he earned All Star designation as the top overall swimmer in his age group.

Writing and Publication

He has written extensively. His publications in the field of swimming include *SwimSwim*, NEM Newsletter, the Brown Swim Newsletter and this full-length instructional book, *Good Swimming*.

Coaching and Other

Wilson has had coaching and informal mentor relationships with hundreds of other Masters swimmers, recreational swimmers, triathletes, and workout swimmers.

Professional Marathon Swimmer

He swam in the Block Island Race in 1950 and the Canadian Exposition (Lake Ontario Swim) in Toronto, Canada, in 1950.

Brown University

He was the top middle distance swimmer. By the time of his graduation, he held university records in four events—220-yard freestyle, 440-yard freestyle, 1,500 freestyle, and a share of the 400-freestyle relay. He was voted Most Valuable Swimmer in 1950.

Honors

He is an inductee in the following halls of fame: Brown University Athletic Hall of Fame, Rhode Island Aquatics Hall of Fame, and the International Scholar Athlete Hall of Fame.

GOOD SWIMMING VIDEO

Be the best you can be!

Get the competitive edge!

This video will help!

Elite swimmer, Mike Lane, demonstrates each stroke, both above and below the surface of the water. The pictures are clear and easy to follow. The running time at normal speed is slightly over five minutes. The slow motion and stop action features are extremely helpful!

Send check or money order for $19.95 (includes shipping and handling) to Consumer Concepts, LLC, P.O. Box 1036, Coventry, Rhode Island 02816. Inquiries at consumer_conceptsllc@yahoo.com or 401 301-7022..

Get Published, Inc!
Thorofare, NJ 08086
06 January, 2009
BA2010006